MW01701168

The M.E.S.S. We Made

Understanding the Four Make or Break Pillars of Love and Life

J. Michael Grey

Table of Contents

About the Author

J. Michael Grey is an accomplished professional with a dynamic career trajectory, who has had an incredible career as a trained Marriage and Family Therapist and Certified Professional Life Coach and now a prominent role in Higher Education. He now applies his extensive coaching expertise to guide the welfare of serval coaching clients and approximately 37,000 students along with numerous staff and faculty members.

His previous experience dealing with mental health directly informs his work and allows him to integrate his passion for human behavior into his daily practices. He is a coach, speaker, educator, and a forever student always learning as life continues to teach many valuable lessons through his personal life and his professional experiences.

A compassionate friend, a proud parent, a loving person. He is someone who followed and now leads; someone who has had success and made mistakes; someone just like you. Jay believes no one is perfect, but all people should be putting in a valiant effort to grow, build back families and society, and realize a better present and future.

Through this book, he hopes to support or spark the improvement of relationships by promoting education, understanding, and the profound power of the pillars: M.E.S.S.

Introduction

Love does not consist of gazing at each other, but in looking together in the same direction. —Antoine de Saint-Exupéry

He Said, She Said

Carter and Tanya have been together for three years. For the most part, their relationship has been going pretty steady, except they have struggled to deepen their love as the years have gone by. The reason for this is that they often love hard and fight hard. When there is peace and stability in their union, the couple feels connected to each other. However, as soon as one of them is caught in the wrong, asked to compromise, or feels triggered in any way, the energy between them shifts, and their relationship becomes a battleground.

There is no doubt that Carter and Tanya are in love, but their love for one another comes with terms and conditions, such as:

- "You will give me anything I want."
- "I won't do anything that takes me outside of my comfort zone."

- "I can't accept your beliefs if they are different from mine."
- "Making mistakes is unforgivable."
- "You need to make me happy."
- "I need access to you every minute of the day."
- "I will emotionally shut down if I don't get what I need."
- "The option to break up with you is always on the table."

Romantic relationships that come with such rigid terms and conditions tend to spiral down the destructive path of pointing fingers, victimhood, denial, gaslighting, and seeking to win arguments rather than resolving them. Even though it is expected for couples to enter relationships with expectations and different views, the challenge they face is learning how to fight constructively, in a manner that doesn't chip away at the trust formed and deepens love and intimacy between them in the long term.

Cleaning Up the M.E.S.S

Perfect relationships don't exist because perfect partners don't exist. You might be in a relationship with someone who ticks many of your boxes; however, they won't always show up in ways you expect.

Similar to you, your partner has a unique perspective on relationships that is shaped by their beliefs, values, and history. Sometimes, what they need and want from the relationship may come as a surprise or feel offensive to you. To get on the same page with them, without turning your differences into arguments, you will need to openly share your thoughts and feelings and be willing to hear and empathize with where they are coming from.

Experts always say that communication is the number one skill for couples to learn in romantic relationships. However, I believe that the "make-or-break" skill that all couples ought to learn is how to fight constructively. Let's face it—you won't always feel madly in love with your partner, especially when they push your buttons. But the low moments you encounter should not reach a stage where they threaten the stability of your union.

A powerful relationship-building strategy that I have created, and often shared with my coaching clients who desire to learn how to fight constructively and love intentionally, is M.E.S.S. The acronym outlines four pillars (i.e. Mental, Emotional, Sexual, and Spiritual pillars) for building resilient and healthy relationships.

For many singles and couples, the internet (and particularly social media) has become the go-to source for receiving dating and marriage advice. Gone are the days when individuals consulted with their parents or grandparents, read books from trained therapists, or joined social clubs to network and meet like-minded people. It is far more entertaining and convenient to scroll up and listen to 15-second love advice, given by someone who looks like you and has probably been through similar experiences.

However , not all dating advice is created equal and many of these people have little to no positive experience or training and tend to just simply reinforce old narratives, stereotypes, and troupes that often sets unrealistic expectations about relationships that don't match reality. Worst of all, if you scroll through 20 posts and notice that everybody is saying the same thing, you are more likely to believe it is true.

So, what exactly is social media saying about love and intimacy? Here are three examples of bad dating advice I have come across—perhaps you have heard them too:

1. **Play hard to get. Don't show your partner how much you are interested in them.**

   In the virtual world, dating is often treated like a game of who can outsmart and gain an advantage over the other person. This type of mentality is responsible for the manipulative tactics that are often used in the early stages of getting to know someone, such as hot-and-cold texting, hiding your intentions, carrying out tests, and keeping scores. The consequence of playing these tactics is that couples struggle to build trust and create a safe environment to be vulnerable and get to know each other.

2. **You will instantly connect with your soulmate. They will be intuitive about what you need.**

   Another problematic piece of advice often given online is to expect a strong connection with your partner from the onset, and when it isn't there, this is seen as a lack of compatibility. Related to this, singles and couples are told that the "right one" will intuitively know what they need and take action. It is unrealistic to expect your partner to be a mind-reader or for your new relationship to feel solid within the first months of getting to know each other. There isn't a standard timeline for building a strong connection with your partner; for some people, it can be instant, while for others it can take years. With that said, at the foundation of a strong connection is open communication, so without feeling safe to share your thoughts and feelings with your significant other, you cannot establish that passionate intimacy.

3. **If he or she doesn't want the same things as you, move on. They are not the right partner.**

   One of the pressures placed on modern relationships is the need for couples to share the same beliefs and outlook on life and dating. This goes beyond searching for someone with similar values as you (an age-old piece of advice that has been proven to work). The danger of following this advice is that oftentimes good men and women are rejected simply because they disagree or have slightly different views than their counterparts. Silly differences like – "How much to spend on first date or Who do they think is right in this argument I heard about from a friend?" Couples who have adopted this mentality may argue whenever they cannot seem to mutually agree on a way forward, and neither party feels they should compromise.

M.E.S.S is a counter-culture tool that both couples and singles looking for love can use to understand what makes healthy romantic relationships. It seeks to cut through the noise of social media and offer you advice backed up with scientific evidence. What makes M.E.S.S stand out from other dating and marriage techniques is that it considers the fact that relationships are unions built by two separate individuals, who have unique needs and desires. Healthy relationships require open and honest communication around topics that matter most to both individuals, such as mental, emotional, sexual, and spiritual well-being.

Having worked as a professional Marriage and Family Therapist for many years before transitioning into the educational sector, I have had the pleasure of working with dozens of couples and teaching them how to clean up the M.E.S.S in their relationships. It has brought me so much joy to watch couples who couldn't even look at each other when they started therapy sessions leave with a greater appreciation for each other and a renewed commitment to their unions.

Throughout the book, you will get to hear some of the success stories that have come from the M.E.S.S program, so you can hopefully be inspired to embark on this journey with your significant other. Tear-jerking testimonials aside, this book also promises to teach you basic interpersonal skills that can help you communicate effectively, learn the art of negotiation, empathize with your partner, and develop a genuine and lifelong connection with your partner.

Are you ready to transform how you think about dating and marriage? If so, *the M.E.S.S Masterclass starts now!*

Chapter 1:

The Foundation of M.E.S.S

You don't develop courage by being happy in your relationships every day. You develop it by surviving difficult times and challenging adversity. —Epicurus

The State of Modern Love

Have you ever wondered where your dating preferences come from? For instance, were you born being drawn to a certain type of personality? Are your dating beliefs based on childhood experiences or past failed relationships?

Social conditioning, the unconscious cultural training that individuals in society go through, plays a big role in molding your views about relationships. The training starts at home by observing your family dynamics and picking up unconscious messages about what social interactions should look like. These unconscious messages are also passed down through school, sports, social gatherings, and the media.

As a result, every generation has its unique ideas and beliefs about the nature of relationships between the sexes that were largely informed by social conditioning and cultural norms at the time. If you were to ask an elderly person to share stories about their teenage dating experiences, they would sound different from what you would hear from a young person today. This is because the society that Gen X and Baby Boomers were born into isn't the same as the society that has raised Gen Z and Millennials.

Therefore, when we talk about "modern love" or "modern relationships," we describe the current social and cultural trends or norms that influence how singles find love and how couples maintain their relationships. This doesn't mean that traditional values have been tossed out of the window; however, they are less dominant today than they were a century ago. In other words, if you follow traditional dating codes, you choose a path that not many people are familiar with or have chosen to follow.

To understand the state of modern love, it is important to consider social factors that have transformed culture, such as the invention of digital technology. With the popularity of computers, software, and smart devices, social networking is something that is predominantly practiced online rather than in person. Gone are the days of sending postcards or meeting people face-to-face to build relationships. Calls and messaging can be done instantaneously, which has changed the meaning of socializing.

With technological disruptions taking place across the world, the nature of dating and finding true love have also received a system update, and here's how:

Online Dating

Many years ago, the easiest way to meet potential partners was to go to bars and restaurants or join social clubs and organizations. Eventually, online dating apps and websites were invented, and they simplified matchmaking by giving you access to a dating pool of singles on your phone.

When online dating sites were introduced, they came with several benefits. The first is that it made dating more convenient. You didn't have to buy a concert ticket or pay for drinks at a club to meet someone amazing; you could simply swipe left or right on your phone.

Another benefit of social media and dating apps was that they allowed each user to build a profile that shared a little about themselves. This meant that you could filter through people you liked or disliked quicker than if you were to meet each individual in real life and get to know them organically. You could also craft the perfect picture of yourself which definitely brought along both good and bad.

Even though online dating has made it more convenient to find love, some might argue that it has also led to the decline of genuine connections. The swiping mechanism and influence of algorithms to find compatible matches have increased expectations when it comes to finding the right partner.

Users get into the habit of searching for people who match their interests, career and educational levels, financial status, attractiveness, and ambitions, and due to this, the emphasis for many people has been on finding partners whom they, on a superficial level, share similarities with. They typically discover major red flags and incompatibilities as they get to know each other beyond external qualities.

Online dating has also promoted unrealistic relationship standards and given singles hope that the "perfect partner" exists and can be found after a few more swipes. This has created a sense of entitlement in modern dating, where individuals are less willing to compromise on their preferences or negotiate the terms of a relationship. In relationships, couples are less tolerant of one another and are more likely to call it quits without attempting to discuss and work out differences.

Commitment Issues

The ability to find instant love, with minimal effort invested, has led to an increase in commitment issues. A report compiled by the Pew Research Center found that Millennials (classified as individuals between the ages of 18 and 34) are less likely to be married in their 20s than previous generations due to having an overwhelming amount of choice when it comes to choosing a mate, amongst other factors (Landau, 2016).

The logic, for many people, is simple: *Why settle for the first person you meet when you can potentially meet your soulmate in a week or a month from now?*

Moreover, since many relationships are initiated and maintained virtually, there is less pressure for couples to physically meet, formalize their unions, and go through the normal growth stages of a relationship. As a result, many modern romantic relationships remain stuck in the initial getting-to-know or honeymoon stage and cannot mature into meaningful connections. Virtual dating also makes it easier for couples to break up or for one person to disappear and exit the relationship due to a lack of being physically accountable to their significant other.

Circling back to the subject of choice, democratized dating has caused many to fear commitment and avoid long-term relationships. The idea of having to be responsible and deal with 'real life' and the highs and lows makes people even more reluctant to commit to the real thing. Traditionally, the purpose of dating was to get married and start a family, but that is not how society defines dating today. Nowadays, dating is about meeting new people who complement your lifestyle. This could mean dating multiple people simultaneously, who each have something different to offer.

Love Bombing

One of the drawbacks of not being able to physically connect with your love interest and gauge how you feel around them is that you can fall victim to "pretend love" or what is commonly referred to as love bombing. On the surface, the love bombing looks like genuine intimacy; however, it is a manipulation tactic used by opportunists to lower your psychological defenses and take advantage of you.

We can define love bombing as providing an excessive amount of attention and affection early in a relationship to manipulate the other person's emotions and control their behaviors. The reason why love bombing has become common in the modern dating world is that many people get to know each other over the internet and cannot follow the natural processes of getting to know someone.

It is hard to tell over texts, phone calls, or video calls if you are compatible with someone and whether your connection is genuine or not. Your potential love interest can tell lies, exaggerate aspects of their life, and make false promises, and you wouldn't be able to know if what you are being told is true. Manipulative people use love bombing as a strategy to create an illusion of true love so that their unsuspecting victims can fall for their tricks and agree to move the relationship along, against their better judgment. Let's be honest, we have all seen the Instagram pictures with 5000 roses, Louis Vuitton boxes and roof top dinner for a Valentine's Day post but does this person have the willingness, commitment, or ability to sustain these behaviors or other behaviors that express true genuine agape love the other 364 days of the year.

The speed at which society is progressing is rapid, and so is the speed at which individuals are getting into relationships and falling in love. For instance, it is common to hear stories of couples getting married after three months of knowing each other, even though science finds that it takes 14 months to know a person (Popova & Wiese, 2022). Couples who rush the dating process are at a higher risk of being deceived by manipulators or committing to people they have not fully vetted for red flags or incompatibilities.

The Idea of the "Perfect Partner"

Comparison culture on social media has impacted the way singles choose their partners and the level of satisfaction couples feel about their relationships. Before social media existed, ideas and expectations about dating were influenced by the family unit, church, and small community. For instance, a young lady would dream of getting married to a spouse with similar traits as her father or priest. Her insight into male behavior and expectations was limited to the few male figures she had been exposed to.

When social media was invented, it connected people from all walks of life and challenged socially acceptable norms and behaviors. People who were raised in small towns could get a glimpse of the lifestyle of city dwellers, and those who came from conservative backgrounds could learn from people with liberal and unconventional views. As you can imagine, this impacted how people approach dating. For example, instead of the young lady looking for a male partner with personality traits similar to her father or priest, she may raise the bar (as encouraged by her social media community) and search for a partner who displays idealistic traits.

Terms like "high-value man" and "high-value woman" are part of the reason why many people believe that the ideal partner exists. It is common for singles to look for potential partners who embody desirable masculine or feminine traits that complement their personalities in relationships. However, unrealistic expectations are created when extreme forms of masculinity and femininity are pushed and seen to be the standard when choosing a romantic partner.

For example, instead of searching for men who are providers, which is a realistic standard, some single women today look for men who earn salaries within a certain high-income bracket (i.e. six or seven figures). Even though men who fit these criteria exist, they are a minority, and therefore, creating a standard based on income can be seen as unrealistic.

Added to this, social media often bombards users with images and videos of "perfect partners" who become the type of partner that everybody strives to be with. For example, the perfect man tends to be depicted as someone who has achieved financial freedom and can spoil his significant other. In photos and videos, this man is seen driving sports cars, traveling the world with his partner, and buying her expensive gifts. While such gentlemen exist, they are rare. Furthermore, this type of representation excludes a large majority of good men who are still working toward achieving financial security.

The perfect woman, on the other hand, is depicted on social media as a hypersexual or goddess-like beautiful woman who fits the role of a trophy wife or stay-at-home mother. Women who fit this idealistic standard exist, but once again, they are rare. Furthermore, this type of representation excludes a large majority of good women who may not fit Western standards of beauty. Seeing these images and representations on social media can create commitment issues and insecurities when searching for love due to the fear of missing out on landing the dream man or woman.

The factors mentioned above are just a few of the modern trends and norms influencing how people approach love and dating. Reflect on how you may have encountered these factors in your love life and how they have influenced your ideas about dating.

The Ripple Effect

You may be wondering how and when the relationship dynamic between men and women started to change. The shift from traditional to modern romantic relationships began in the 19th century and continued into the 20th century. During these years, ideologies that challenged the status quo and traditional gender and societal norms became prominent. The following sections will look at three examples of social changes that redefined roles within relationships and changed the way couples approached dating and marriage.

Patriarchy vs. Feminism

The patriarchal system that modern society is built upon was founded between 8,000-3,000 BC. The word "patriarchy," which means "the rule of the father," is an old institution whereby men dominate all spheres of society. For thousands of years, the system allowed men special privileges to control the means of production and play an instrumental role in the development of civilization, including the formation of the family unit.

Patriarchal gender roles created a power imbalance in romantic relationships between men and women. Men were seen as the providers who went outside the home to find work and bring in money. Women were seen as caregivers who raised children and took care of the household. While women still performed work inside the home, it didn't afford them the same economic power men had. Society assigned men the role of leadership in relationships, and women were subjugated to their control.

During the mid-19th century, a new social movement known as feminism emerged, intending to seek more social and political opportunities for women. Hundreds of women across the Western world united to fight for gender equality. In the span of four waves, the movement challenged patriarchal gender roles like the domestication of women, fought for sexual and reproductive rights, and challenged the concept of femininity and womanhood.

Feminism empowered women to question and challenge the power imbalance in romantic relationships. They wanted the same privileges men had enjoyed for centuries, such as the privilege to go outside the home and work, the privilege to speak up and feel their opinions mattered, and the privilege to communicate their standards and expectations in a relationship without being labeled as difficult or aggressive.

The movement gave rise to generations of women who refused to conform to traditional gender roles. They wanted to be seen and treated as equals by their significant others, instead of subordinates. New relationship norms, influenced by the feminist movement, began to emerge in the 20th century. These included:

- **Seeking consent:** To show respect for partners' physical, mental, and emotional boundaries, couples are encouraged to ask questions and understand what their loved ones deem acceptable or unacceptable behaviors. For example, instead of grabbing your partner's hand, assuming they are comfortable with that kind of touch, you are encouraged to discuss their preferences relating to physical displays of affection.

- **Equitable partnerships:** Traditionally, women were expected to do most of the emotional labor in a relationship, such as checking on their partner and offering support. Nowadays, this is a responsibility that both men and women share. Modern relationships are built on reciprocity, which is the balance of give and take. Men and women are required to be emotionally available for their significant others for the union to thrive.

- **Honest communication:** Feminism challenged stereotypes about how men and women communicate with each other. For instance, men had rich emotional lives similar to women, and it was important for them to feel safe sharing their thoughts and feelings (rather than seeing it as a weakness). On the other hand, women's voices were seen as powerful, and they were encouraged to be more assertive in setting boundaries and expressing their needs.

The goal of feminism is to free both men and women from an oppressive patriarchal system that assigns rigid gender roles. Modern couples are redefining what it means to be girlfriend/boyfriend or wife/husband, and seeking to build relationships that play to each individual's strengths. This has improved communication and negotiation skills between couples and enabled them to decide on how to structure their relationships and relate with one another.

Just like with all things, both positive and negatives have spun out of these historical changes but the initial purpose behind it truly has affected the dating world today. While extremism has become prevalent on both sides there are moral principles that at the core we can all agree upon.

Religion vs. Secularism

Traditional societies used religion to promote ethics, enforce moral codes, and set standards for legal behaviors. In the West, Judaism and Christianity were the predominant religions followed whereas in the East, Islam, Hinduism, and Buddhism were (and largely still) influence the culture of most societies.

Religious ideas have played an important role in defining acceptable and unacceptable behaviors between men and women. For example, in many religions, dating (known as courting) is a short period where a man and a woman get to know each other and see whether they are compatible to be married. Sexual acts are not permitted, since they are seen as a privilege for married couples.

Another common relationship expectation promoted by many religions is the need to procreate and start a family. The ultimate purpose of dating is to find a suitable wife or husband and get married. From an early age, men and women are taught to desire to have children and start families. This is seen as the highest social honor and display of manhood and womanhood.

The role and significance of religion in modern society have been challenged due to the growing number of secular ideas, norms, and beliefs. Many people who were followers of particular religions have fallen away and chosen instead to align with minority groups and movements that are relevant to their needs and experiences. Countries like the UK and the US that were once in favor of Christianity are now gradually moving toward secularism, where they promote the beliefs and freedoms of all citizens, regardless of age, sex, gender, race, culture, and religion.

In secular societies, all schools of thought are welcome. This means that romantic relationships can be defined and experienced in unique ways. Gone are the days when marriage was seen to be a rite of passage for young people or monogamy was seen as the only acceptable type of relationship between couples. Moreover, with communities like the LGBTQIA+ becoming larger and more vocal about their needs and beliefs, society has been forced to look beyond heterosexual norms when exploring dating and marriage.

Many singles and couples are also starting to question the relevance of traditional morals and ethics, often based on religious principles. For example, the idea of withholding sex until marriage seems irrelevant to somebody who isn't religious or doesn't desire to get married. Similarly, being intimate with multiple partners isn't considered socially unacceptable or sinful to somebody who is polyamorous.

Modern dating rules and norms promote freedom of choice rather than a particular ideology. The decision about whether something is good or bad is left to each individual to make. It is therefore more common to find couples who have different beliefs and outlooks on life coming together to make a relationship work. To avoid arguments about who's wrong and who's right, communication and empathy are required.

Community vs. Individualism

Independence can be defined as the freedom to define who you are and how you desire to live. Part of growing up and becoming a responsible adult involves cultivating a sense of independence so that you can stand on your own. However, modern society has taken independence to extreme lengths by promoting individualism.

Independence and individualism may sound like the same concept, but they describe different outlooks on life. An independent person spends time developing their character and learning skills to live a sustainable lifestyle that isn't dependent on the charity and assistance of others. Nonetheless, they are still invested in their community and see the value in networking and collaborating with others to achieve mutual goals.

In contrast, someone who believes in individualism sees themselves as being the center of their world. They take independence to an extreme where only their needs and desires matter. Due to a lack of trust in others, they tend to isolate themselves and focus on achieving goals alone. The fast-paced, competitive nature of modern society has caused many people to adopt the mindset of being self-reliant and hyper-focused on their well-being. It is not common to find people who are looking out for their friends, family, or neighbors because "self-care" has become more important than a sense of community.

The absence of community has impacted how people relate with one another. For example, people often enter romantic relationships with the mentality of having their needs fulfilled, rather than seeking to support and respond to the needs of their significant other. This selfish behavior is rooted in the hyperfocus on "I" and failing to think in terms of "we." Modern love has also become transactional, in that couples often keep scores of what each person brings to the table and how much investment they have made. As a result, relationships can feel competitive instead of supportive.

One of the ways individualism manifests in relationships is in the fear or reluctance to ask for help. This shows a lack of trust in the other person to respond to a need. Alternatively, it could reveal an extreme sense of self-reliance that undermines the partnership. In some cases, individualism increases the risk of narcissistic tendencies in relationships, where one partner lacks empathy and consideration for their counterpart. A study published in the Journal of Social and Personal Relationships found that individualism in romantic relationships led to a game-playing love dynamic where the individualistic person treated the relationship as a means to an end and was obsessively self-focused (Le, 2005).

It is no secret that narcissism is becoming more prevalent in the modern dating world. Nowadays, people are out to get what they want and ignore the fact that they are dealing with human beings who have their own needs and expectations. To build healthy and balanced relationships, it is necessary to return to a sense of community where we show concern and compassion for the well-being of our loved ones.

Looking back at these three major social changes of the 19th and 20th centuries, can you see how your ideas about dating and relationships are influenced by social norms? Think back to how your understanding of dating has evolved over the years alongside the movements and social changes mentioned above.

Upon These Pillars

Even though we live in a society where anything is permissible, there is still a right and wrong way of dating. Getting into a relationship and applying the Do-It-Yourself method can lead to anxiety and heartbreak. Unfortunately, dating isn't something you can improvise because you are dealing with another human being, who enters the partnership with their own unique beliefs, needs, and standards. Unless both of you can get on the same page and openly discuss what type of relationship you want and the best way to achieve that goal, the relationship may soon collapse under pressure.

The objective of the M.E.S.S pillars is to teach you how to create the relationship of your dreams by exploring and discussing four major components to building healthy and long-lasting intimate relationships:

Mental Health

Couples enter relationships with scars from the past. These scars shape their mindset, attitudes, and approach to dating and life. Learning about your partner's past experiences and how they have influenced the person they are today can help you understand why they think and respond to situations in a certain way. Moreover, you can discuss possible emotional triggers, unresolved trauma, and other mental health issues and mentalities constructed from their past that could arise and present challenges in your relationship.

Emotional Health

Every individual, regardless of their background, has a set of needs that they cannot fulfill on their own. They require loving support from their partner to fulfill these needs and feel secure and balanced. One of the commitments couples ought to make early on in their relationship is to be responsive to each other's needs. However, without creating an emotionally safe space to be vulnerable with one another and communicate what these needs are, couples can feel afraid to open up and express their emotions.

Sexual Health

Chemistry in a romantic relationship is crucial for building physical intimacy. However, the chemistry doesn't come instantly for many couples or fades away after the honeymoon stage. For partners to sustain a physical desire for each other in the long term, they need to confront the barriers to physical intimacy like the misalignment of sexual expectations, the effects of past sexual trauma, and being closed off to broader displays of intimacy that go beyond the bedroom.

Spiritual Health

Spirituality transcends religion and describes a holistic connection to yourself. Partners who feel safe opening up to each other and sharing their authentic selves tend to feel happier and more secure in the relationship. To build spiritual intimacy, it is important for couples to feel accepted by their significant others. This enables them to feel comfortable having tough conversations, discussing ideas and beliefs, and imagining a future together.

What's important to note about these pillars is that they are not based on a particular ideology or principle, but instead on what enables two people to connect and cultivate closeness. Think of M.E.S.S as the building blocks of true intimacy that promote trust, openness, and vulnerability.

This book takes an in-depth look at the four pillars of M.E.S.S and seeks to offer guidance on how you can approach these topics of conversations with your partner (or potential partner). To achieve a healthy and fulfilling relationship, your couple's goal should be to align yourself with these pillars and build a strong foundation. The benefit of learning about M.E.S.S is that you will be able to identify imbalances in your relationship or areas where you can improve. This proactive approach to problem-solving can prevent tumultuous arguments, power struggles, and feeling misunderstood by your partner.

If you think of your romantic love as a house, these four pillars are what hold up the structure. In other words, they hold equal weight and play a significant role in keeping your relationship stable and balanced.

An Invitation to Self-Discovery

You have witnessed the dating culture evolve. However, your views and approach to dating have changed too. You may not be as easily trusting or vulnerable in your relationships as you used to be due to past experiences that have shifted your perspective.

Taking an honest look at your dating or marriage journey thus far can help you identify which pillars of M.E.S.S you need to focus on while preparing for your next relationship or when seeking to improve your current relationship. It is easier to point fingers at your ex-partners or current partners and put a spotlight on areas they were lacking. But for your dating life to improve, you must take responsibility for your shortcomings and look for solutions.

The following self-assessment is designed to help you reflect and journal about your dating life and identify which of the four pillars of M.E.S.S you need to improve in your life. Encourage your partner to take this self-assessment too, so that both of you are aware of your starting points and can support one another along the way.

1. What is the average lifespan of your romantic relationships?

____

____

____

____

____

2. What pattern do your romantic relationships tend to follow?

____

3. What is your philosophy about dating/marriage?

4. What are your fears about dating/marriage?

5. What does a successful relationship look like?

6. In what ways has your outlook on relationships changed over the years?

7. When last did you have a heart-to-heart with your partner?

8. What have you learned about your dating habits recently?

9. How do you express love in a relationship?

10. How important is physical intimacy to you?

11. What are your favorite ways to have fun with your partner?

12. Describe three things you need from a relationship.

Chapter 2:

Mental Matters in Love

You can talk with someone for years, every day, and still, it won't mean as much as what you can have when you sit in front of someone, not saying a word, yet you feel that person with your heart, you feel like you have known the person for forever. —C. JoyBell C.

The Mind's Impact

The first pillar of M.E.S.S is Mental Health. Your mental health refers to your psychological well-being, which is influenced by how you think and feel about yourself and the world around you. To assess the state of your mental health, you are encouraged to examine the quality of your thoughts, emotions, and behaviors, and how these elements interact with each other.

In psychology, thoughts, emotions, and behaviors are seen as being interlinked. An idea comes into your mind as a thought and triggers a specific emotional reaction that ultimately compels you to take action. This process works the same for positive and negative thoughts; a positive thought leads to positive emotions and behaviors, and a negative thought leads to negative emotions and behaviors.

Your mental health is also shaped by your mindset, the set of beliefs and attitudes that help you make sense of the world. Everybody has a mindset, but not every mindset leads to productive and positive thinking. There are some mindsets, like the scarcity mindset, that reinforce ideas of lack and limited resources. People who have adopted this mindset tend to be overthinkers and feel intense anxiety about the possibility of running out of resources or forfeiting opportunities.

What's interesting about mindsets is that they can evolve or change in different contexts. For example, your mindset toward one area of your life may not be the same as your mindset toward another area of your life. Take, for example, your career and love life. When it comes to your career, you may display a growth mindset, which refers to the belief that your skills and knowledge can deepen and become better over time. Possessing this type of mindset can help you learn from your mistakes and have a positive response to challenges.

However, when it comes to your love life, you may display a fixed mindset, which refers to the belief that your traits and abilities are fixed and cannot develop. Whenever you are confronted with challenges, you turn to solutions that have worked in the past instead of looking for new ways to solve interpersonal problems. Furthermore, you may be reluctant to confront your bad habits or attitudes, even when they start to compromise the health of your relationship, due to believing they form part of who you are and cannot be changed.

Updating Your Mental Model

You may be wondering what mental health and mindsets have to do with building strong romantic relationships. How you think about partnership determines how you feel, and eventually, how you behave, in your romantic relationships.

When you get into a relationship, you have ideas and beliefs about what to expect. These ideas and beliefs are informed by your mindset and personal history. For example, if you have a history of being lied to by your ex-partners, you might develop a belief that nobody can be trusted.

Based on your ideas and beliefs, you are triggered to feel certain emotions and behave in certain ways. Having a history of being lied to, for example, could make you feel suspicious of your romantic partner's motives. As a result of feeling this way, it may take a lot of time and convincing before you can open up to them.

Knowing how to make the association between your thoughts, emotions, and behaviors, and examine the impact of your current mindset on your romantic relationships, can help you discover and update your mental model. How you approach dating is not random. It is based on a particular mental framework that helps you process information, solve complex problems, and make informed decisions.

Whenever you are confronted with a situation that is similar to what you have experienced before, your brain takes a shortcut and refers to a mental model related to that area of your life. This explains why your romantic relationships often follow the same patterns and lead to the same outcomes; the same methods of thinking are used to evaluate and make decisions about every relationship, regardless of how different the circumstances may be.

To build strong relationships, it is vital to revisit your mental models and assess whether your mindset helps or harms your general outlook and approach. Consider how much of your mental framework is based on disempowering beliefs and attitudes rooted in past trauma and failure. The only way to cultivate healthy love is to possess healthy ideas and beliefs about love.

Echoes of the Past

One of the best places to start when updating your mental model about relationships is by reflecting on the past. Many of your beliefs about love and intimacy were formed during those first encounters, receiving affection from other people. As a child, the most important relationship in your life was the relationship with your parents. Second to that was the relationships formed with your extended family, teachers, classmates, and of course, your first real boyfriend or girlfriend.

When you were a young child, you didn't know what love meant. The only way to tell if somebody loved you was by watching how they treated you. At different stages of childhood and adolescence, you require your parents and community to respond to certain needs. For instance, as an infant, you had simple survival needs like being fed, washed, comforted, and put to sleep.

The older you grew, the more complex your needs became. Beyond physical security, you need emotional security shown through behaviors like being listened to, treated with respect, and having your feelings validated. During adolescence, when you began to break away from your parents and develop a separate identity, you relied on your circle of friends, emotional support from teachers, and validation from your high school love interest to feel secure and confident in who you are.

If your needs were never met or only met on some occasions, you may have developed childhood trauma. We can define childhood trauma as any event or experience that causes pain or distress for a child and leaves an emotional wound. The event or experience is interpreted by the child as scary, violent, dangerous, or overwhelming. There are different forms of childhood trauma, such as physical, sexual, and emotional abuse. However, another type of trauma that is often overlooked is childhood emotional neglect, which occurs when parents fail to respond or behave appropriately to their children's emotional needs.

Childhood trauma can also be caused by events and experiences outside the home, such as being bullied at school, experiencing public humiliation, or being rejected by your peer group or the high school boyfriend or girlfriend you cared about. These events and experiences may not necessarily leave physical scars, but they can affect your psychological well-being to the extent of changing the way you think and interact with people.

The Impact of Trauma on Adult Relationships

The pain and difficulties from the past may be distant memories, but they impact your mental model about relationships. As a child, you didn't have an explanation for why some of the negative events or experiences were happening in your life. In the absence of answers, you came up with your assumptions about what was happening and found ways to cope that were not always helpful.

Once I had a couple come into my office to see me about relationship problems they were experiencing. A major problem they had was managing conflict. The lady, let's call her Susan, tended to yell whenever she felt upset. Triggered by his partner's yelling, the gentleman, let's call him David, would immediately shut down.

We spent many weeks exploring their childhoods and discovered why both of them responded to conflict in their respective ways. Susan was raised by a controlling mother who managed every aspect of her life until she ran away from home at the age of 16. As a child and teenager, she never felt respected and accepted for who she was.

As a result of her upbringing, Susan developed a disdain for authority. Whenever she felt misunderstood or criticized, she would respond with an explosion reaction. In her eyes, this response helped her correct a perceived power imbalance. This was how she made sense of her mother's control tactics as a child, and the best way she knew how to cope.

David was raised by emotionally unavailable parents. Throughout his childhood, he tried different ways to seek their approval and feel loved. Gaining his parents' approval made him feel good about himself, but being ignored by them made him feel guilty and inadequate. Even though his parents had their reasons for not being emotionally available for their son, David blamed himself and responded by emotionally shutting down.

Here is a couple struggling to manage conflict, and still dealing with the impact of past trauma. How they interpret events taking place in their relationship is through the eyes of the little girl and little boy who survived a painful upbringing. By confronting their childhood wounds and going through the healing process together, both Susan and David learned to regulate their emotions and triggers and respond differently in conflict situations.

Trauma-Based Responses to Be Mindful Of

Growing up and moving away from home doesn't erase childhood trauma. There are many couples today who continue to respond to everyday relationship challenges with trauma-abased responses, as a result of not healing from past hurts.

Trauma-based responses are behaviors that stem from unresolved emotional wounds. Remember the connection between thoughts, emotions, and behaviors? Well, trauma-based responses occur whenever there are lingering negative beliefs and emotions rooted in past painful experiences.

Consider the following beliefs:

- It's not safe to open up.
- Everyone is out to get me.
- My feelings don't matter.
- Crying is a sign of weakness.
- I have to change to be accepted.

Have these thoughts ever crossed your mind? If you were to investigate where these beliefs come from, you would be transported back to past situations that made you feel rejected, betrayed, or invalidated. Whenever challenges in your adult romantic relationships trigger these beliefs, the pain from the past resurfaces, and you respond with trauma-based coping behaviors.

The chain of events goes like this:

Negative trauma-based belief = Emotional trigger = Trauma-based response

What's important to understand about trauma-based responses is that they are valid coping mechanisms, despite being harmful to your well-being and detrimental to your intimate relationships. You respond with those trauma-based coping behaviors because, on a subconscious level, that is what you believe is the best choice of action. Other underlying psychological problems that might cause you to respond in that particular way are battling mental health conditions like anxiety, depression, or post-traumatic stress disorder (PTSD).

Trauma-based responses look different for every individual; however, here are examples of how you might respond when you are emotionally triggered:

1. Exaggerated emotional response to minor relationship inconveniences

2. Being afraid or avoiding conflict and confrontation

3. Emotionally withdrawing or shutting down when feeling stressed

4. Making negative assumptions about your partner's choices and behaviors

5. The constant fear of being rejected or abandoned by your partner

6. Difficulty believing that your partner loves you despite receiving ongoing reassurance

7. Being intolerant of your partner's mistakes; expecting them to act right all the time

8. Needing space and time alone; becoming restless and irritable when you are always around your partner

9. Ignoring your partner's red flags; choosing to stay and work things out when the relationship has become toxic

10. Needing to fix, rescue, or change your partner; projecting your feelings of low self-worth on your partner

Reflecting on the examples listed above, how much of a role does your past, as well as your partner's past, play in your relationship? If you discover signs of unaddressed trauma in your relationship, it is important to treat it as a problem affecting both of you, since one person's trauma becomes a serious barrier to intimacy and healthy love in your relationship. With the appropriate therapeutic interventions, you can process and heal the trauma as a couple and strengthen your relationship.

Contending With Cognitive Conundrums

Trauma-based responses cannot be rooted out by simply deciding to adopt new habits. To bring effective change, you must address the faulty thinking that initiated the chain reaction of emotions and behaviors. This means identifying and examining your negative beliefs or assumptions that stem from past experiences.

Cognitive distortions are thinking errors that occur whenever factual information is absent. To make sense of what is happening, your brain refers to established mental models and the interpretation of past events to conclude. Your brain creates an argument that seems convincing, even though it isn't based on truth. Believing your cognitive distortions reinforces negative thinking patterns and can sometimes trigger strong emotions. Thus, to prevent trauma-based responses, it is critical to start by correcting your thinking.

In your romantic relationships, cognitive distortions can show up in various ways, such as:

1. **Assuming the worst-case scenario**

If you have a history of being let down by others, you may develop a habit of jumping to the worst conclusions when you don't have the facts about a situation. For instance, when your partner takes longer to reply to your text messages, you might assume they are intentionally ignoring you. When your partner fails to meet expectations, you might see this as a possible red flag rather than an opportunity to communicate your needs.

2. **Shifting the responsibility for your feelings**

Strong emotions are sometimes difficult to process because they bring a lot of shame, guilt, and disappointment. To avoid feeling bad about yourself, you may tend to make your partner responsible for your feelings. Shifting the responsibility for your feelings may sound like "You make me angry" or "If it wasn't for your actions, I wouldn't feel angry." This type of thinking strips you of the power to control and manage your own emotions and leaves you in a vulnerable and desperate state.

3. **Catastrophizing minor situations**

A clear sign of living with PTSD is having an exaggerated emotional response to minor situations. For example, when your partner uses an exclamation mark at the end of a sentence, you might interpret this as an aggressive tone and respond with defensive behavior. Or when your partner says, "I need time alone," you might interpret this as a sign of rejection or think that you are being punished for doing something to offend them.

4. **Keeping mental scores**

Another trauma-based response in relationships is being obsessed with making things fair (according to your definition). Perhaps in past relationships, you were mistreated and suffered severely for it, and now you are hypervigilant about being taken for granted. To prevent the past from repeating itself, you may keep mental scores about what you do for your partner and what they do for you, expecting them to match every action. This type of thinking creates unrealistic expectations of your partner and can breed resentment.

5. **Invalidating your partner's viewpoint**

Unresolved trauma can cause narrow-minded thinking and confirmation bias, whereby any ideas that don't support your beliefs and values are deemed incorrect. Having this type of mindset can make it difficult to acknowledge differences between you and your partner and validate their point of view, regardless of whether you agree with them or not. During conflict situations, you may downplay your partner's emotional needs or hold onto your position even when you have been shown errors in your thinking.

Cognitive distortions are common in any type of relationship, and the good news is they can be corrected. The most important step to correcting your cognitive distortions is acknowledging that you may not always interpret situations appropriately. At times, your opinions about a situation could be filtered through your personal history, fears, biases, and trauma. Admitting this to yourself isn't easy; however, it can help you confront thinking errors that often trigger negative emotions and behaviors.

Steps to Practice Cognitive Restructuring

Cognitive restructuring is a technique that can help you as individuals, and as a couple, acknowledge, confront, and adjust cognitive distortions. The technique encourages you to explore and ask questions about your beliefs and assumptions instead of treating them as the truth. Doing this allows you to weigh the pros and cons of your thinking and identify possible errors you have made.

Cognitive restructuring is not about judging yourself for entertaining bad thoughts, but rather helping yourself see things from multiple perspectives before concluding. In the absence of facts, you can accept different suggestions and reach a conclusion that is fair, and balanced and deepens your love and understanding for your partner.

There are seven steps you can follow when practicing cognitive restructuring that can lead you to positive thinking outcomes:

Step 1: Describe the situation.

Explain the situation to yourself using objective language. Focus on the factual events that have taken place moments ago. Ask questions like: *What happened? Who was there? How did the situation unfold?*

Example: My partner brushed me off while I was trying to express my feelings.

Step 2: State what you thought.

Soon after witnessing what happened, a thought popped into your mind. What was the thought?

Example: My partner doesn't care about my feelings.

Step 3: Express how this thought made you feel.

As we have discovered, thoughts trigger emotions. Reflect on how you felt when the thought crossed your mind. Remind yourself that your partner is not responsible for your emotions; your emotional experience is a response to how you make sense of what is happening. The only thing your partner can be held responsible for is their actions.

Example: I feel undermined, dismissed, and unappreciated.

Step 4: Find evidence that supports your thought.

Look for evidence that validates the accuracy of your thought. For instance, there may have been scenarios in the past when your assumptions had been true. You can also identify behaviors exhibited by your partner that make your statement true.

Example: Whenever I attempt to have serious conversations, my partner shuts down or becomes defensive.

Step 5: Find evidence that goes against the thought.

Shift your perspective and look for evidence that proves that your thought is inaccurate. For instance, refer to past situations where your partner has responded in loving and positive ways. You can also identify personality traits and behaviors displayed by your partner that make your statement false.

Example: My partner always reassures me of his love through words of affirmation and acts of service. He also makes an effort to comfort me when I am upset.

Step 6: Come up with a fair and balanced thought.

Now that you have the context of the situation and can see both sides of the argument, you have more information at your disposal to make an informed assumption about what was taking place. To balance the evidence that supports and goes against the original thought, take a moment to empathize with your partner. Imagine that they had good intentions for taking certain actions, despite the negative outcome.

Example: Due to my partner's upbringing, he struggles to express emotions or show vulnerability. Shutting down was his way of de-escalating the situation and protecting himself. I know he loves me through his actions and ongoing support.

Step 7: Describe the outcome of adjusting your thinking.

Finally, give yourself feedback after adjusting your thinking. Consider changes that have occurred to your mental well-being and between you and your partner. This final step is supposed to encourage you to trust in the process of cognitive restructuring.

Example: Adjusting my thinking made me feel calm and relieved. It also reminded me of why I love my partner so much!

Synchronizing Minds

The benefit of working together with your partner to address mental health issues is that you can get on the same page without having to change each other. Your partner gains a better understanding of your personal history, beliefs, and attitudes that shape your outlook on the world, and vice versa. Slowly, but surely, you can synchronize your minds and learn to show up for each other in a manner that you both can accept.

Every couple has some form of connection that keeps their relationship going. However, not every connection has psychological roots. For example, one couple might feel a connection based on physical intimacy while another couple might feel a connection based on familiarity (i.e. being high school sweethearts). Couples who desire a psychological connection must work on being in sync with their thinking.

Don't get me wrong, you don't need to share similar beliefs or perspectives with your partner to synchronize your minds—you simply need to display an appreciation for how each of you views the world and a willingness to learn from one another. In other words, it isn't about who has the better mindset, but instead, how your opposing mindsets come together and create a synchronized rhythm.

Several years ago, my wife and I reached a crossroads in our marriage. Coming from different backgrounds, we had conflicting beliefs and expectations about what we needed for our partnership. We had to decide to either learn how to navigate our differences and find common ground, or reconsider whether we were meant to be together. Both of us decided to let go of the need to be understood and do our best to understand and empathize with each other. The process took several months, but eventually, we began to appreciate each other and see the opportunity to approach life differently.

Synchronizing your minds in a relationship requires a certain level of emotional intelligence to acknowledge how both of you may think and feel differently and to not allow those differences to become barriers to connection. It involves leaning toward your partner when you feel uncomfortable rather than pulling away and turning obstacles into opportunities to work as a team.

Any couple can learn to become in sync with each other, even when the connection didn't start strong. Remember, what creates synchronicity is openness, curiosity, and appreciation for who your partner is and how they view and respond to the world. Instead of focusing on being understood, shift your focus to being understanding, and encourage your partner to do the same.

The following exercises will help you get started:

Get to Know Each Other

Don't assume that you know everything about your partner. There are ideas that you haven't heard your partner express, memories about their past that you are unaware of, opinions about life, and philosophical ideas that would take you by surprise. Plan dates where you get to know each other better and ask open-ended questions about every topic under the sun. Here are a few questions to consider:

1. What are your priorities outside of work?

2. What are some of your dreams?

3. When you were a child, what did you want to be when you grew up?

4. What are your go-to coping mechanisms when you feel stressed?

5. What are you most proud of about yourself?

6. Describe your relationship with your family.

7. What's one lesson you have learned from a bad breakup?

8. In your opinion, what makes a good partner?

9. What positive habits make a relationship strong?

10. What do you love most about our relationship?

Schedule Mental Check-Ins

To become in sync with your partner, staying tuned into each other's needs is crucial. Since both of you may have busy schedules, you can schedule a short mental check-in during the day to find out how you are both holding up. These check-ins don't need to be long; however, they should be intentional. For example, during a five-minute call, you can take turns responding to the following questions:

- How are you feeling right now?
- What has gone well so far?
- What are you looking forward to?

During the check-in, give your partner full attention and take in what they have to say. Ask questions and show interest in their day and what they may be experiencing. These check-ins should be positive and uplifting, so avoid bringing up topics that may cause either of you to feel stressed.

Practice Gratitude

Showing appreciation for your partner, and feeling appreciated in return, can strengthen your psychological connection. Practicing gratitude is about noticing the good traits, choices, and behaviors that your partner demonstrates. This requires you to pay attention to them and become emotionally invested in their life. Being shown appreciation makes your partner feel competent, confident, and desired by you, which deepens their feelings toward you.

There are many ways to show your partner appreciation. The trick is to learn what type of praise and recognition they like. For example, does your partner love to hear you express gratitude or read kind words from you in a text message or note? Do they feel appreciated when you show physical affection or when you take care of them by doing acts of service? All of these suggestions are examples of how you can show your partner appreciation, and vice versa.

Chapter 3:

Emotional Entanglements

I've learned that people will forget what you said, people will forget what you did, but people will never forget how you made them feel.
—Maya Angelou

Understanding Emotional Baggage

In the previous chapter, we discussed the first pillar of M.E.S.S, Mental Health, and looked at how mindsets and mental models play a role in shaping your beliefs, attitudes, and expectations within romantic relationships. We discovered the association between thoughts, emotions, and behaviors, and examined how cognitive restructuring can help you address negative thoughts and reduce trauma-based responses that impact the well-being of your relationship.

We are now proceeding to the second pillar of M.E.S.S, Emotional Health, which seeks to teach you how to identify and share your emotional needs with your partner and create an emotionally safe space where they can feel comfortable exploring and expressing their emotions too. Both men and women have a full range of emotions that they are capable of experiencing. What's unfortunate is that society has created unspoken restrictions about which emotions men and women are allowed to display.

For example, it is acceptable for men to display aggression because that is seen as being an emotion inherent in every man. However, they are seen as weak (i.e. lose respect from other men and women) when they display sadness or loneliness. Women, on the other hand, are stereotypically seen as being more sensitive than men and prone to feelings of sadness or loneliness. However, when they display aggression similar to men, they are labeled as "hostile," "rude," or "ungovernable."

Even though we cannot change social constructs, we can build relationships that are safe spaces for men and women to freely express how they feel without being judged, rejected, or treated inferior. To successfully achieve this undertaking, greater emotional intelligence (EQ) from both partners is required. We can define EQ as the ability to acknowledge, process, and manage your emotions, and show empathy and compassion toward the emotions of others.

Partners with high EQ are capable of understanding their emotions and how they might impact their behaviors within the relationship. Moreover, they have a greater sense of self-awareness, which makes it easier for them to separate how they feel from how their significant others feel. Partners with high EQ are also capable of feeling emotions without acting upon them. This helps them communicate how they feel with clarity and confidence.

One of the barriers to achieving high EQ is carrying emotional baggage from the past. Emotional baggage is a metaphor to describe unresolved emotional issues that stem from not having your needs met in the past. The emotional baggage serves as a subconscious reminder of not receiving love, respect, support, or acceptance from the people you trusted and cared for the most.

Whenever you enter new romantic relationships, you transfer your baggage onto the next partner, in hopes that they can help you address your unmet needs. The problem with assigning your new partner this immense task is that they are not responsible for healing your past or fulfilling unmet emotional needs. That task belongs to you. Expecting your new partner to manage your emotional baggage causes unnecessary stress and drama in your relationship and robs them of the opportunity to form a genuine connection with you.

Signs of Emotional Baggage

Nobody asks for emotional baggage. It is the trauma that often follows after surviving a difficult upbringing, leaving an abusive relationship, or experiencing loss. Carrying emotional baggage shouldn't be something that you are ashamed of because everybody has a past, and sometimes it takes decades before some people can confront their pasts and close those chapters.

One of the reasons you may be motivated to address your emotional baggage could be to improve the quality of your relationships. It is difficult to connect with someone and experience real intimacy when you are still holding onto emotional issues from past relationships. By dealing with your emotional baggage, once and for all, you can open your heart again to give and receive love.

There are a few tell-tale signs to look out for that reveal you are carrying emotional baggage:

- **Difficulty letting go of the past:** You frequently bring up the past in conversation, make decisions influenced by past events, and hold grudges for people who have caused you pain.

- **Chronic stress and anxiety:** You struggle to regulate your nervous system and feel a sense of peace in your mind and body. You may experience physical symptoms like chronic migraines, mood swings, colds and flu, insomnia, and weight fluctuations.

- **Difficulty forming healthy relationships:** You get caught in the same toxic relationship cycles and attract people who display similar traits to those who have harmed you in the past. You may also struggle to sustain long-term relationships, set healthy boundaries, or show vulnerability in relationships.

- **Negative self-image:** You tend to put yourself down, set unrealistic standards for relationships, feel unworthy of being loved for who you are, and compare your physical appearance or dating life with other people. These behaviors stem from unprocessed feelings of rejection, failure, or coming out of an abusive relationship.

- **Avoidance of emotional intimacy:** Due to harboring raw and unprocessed emotions, you avoid opening up to people and engaging in deep conversations about your life. This could also make you fear commitment, relationship labels, and making someone else an integral part of your life.

- **Self-sabotaging behaviors:** When you feel vulnerable, your knee-jerk reaction is to become defensive, shut down, or distance yourself. These are forms of self-sabotage that cause you to reject love or make it difficult to sustain a healthy and stable relationship.

Take a moment to think about your past dating experiences and how they have been impacted by carrying emotional baggage. Can you identify recurring destructive patterns that make it difficult to sustain a healthy relationship?

The Art of Emotional Communication

Processing emotional baggage isn't something that can be done overnight. It takes months and sometimes years of introspection, therapy, and cultivating EQ, to let go of the baggage you are carrying. However, this doesn't mean that you should put your dating life on hold.

While you are working on processing your emotional baggage, a useful skill to learn is how to communicate your feelings, especially sensitive feelings that you would normally hide from your partner. There are all sorts of conversations you can have within your relationship, but the conversation about emotions, and subsequently needs, is one of the most important ones to have regularly.

To feel satisfied in your relationship, there are certain things you require from your partner, such as affection, positive reinforcement, support, emotional safety, and companionship, to name a few. When your needs are not met, it is natural to feel stressed, anxious, bored, lonely, jealous, and a range of other emotions. Couples rarely explore emotions deep enough to get to the core, unfulfilled needs behind them. If they did, perhaps there would be less arguing and more problem-solving in intimate relationships.

Talking about your emotions may not always fix situations, but it can invite your partner to step inside your world and get a better understanding of who you are and what you need. Understandably, expressing how you feel is not easy and maybe something that takes you outside your comfort zone. However, the benefits outweigh the costs. When you can clearly and respectfully communicate your feelings, and your partner can do the same, you can achieve greater transparency and build a solid foundation of trust in your relationship.

Before you start practicing how to communicate your feelings, there are some negative beliefs related to emotions that you must confront. These negative beliefs stem from your childhood and past relationship experiences where you felt emotionally neglected, dismissed, or abused. Look at the following list and see if you can identify negative beliefs that you still hold to be true:

- Emotions are irrational and not to be trusted.
- Showing my emotions is a sign of weakness.
- Being emotionless gives me more control.
- Emotions like fear and anger are counterproductive.
- If I allow myself to feel sad, I will feel sad forever.
- Good people don't lose their temper, get jealous, or feel bitterness.

- People will take advantage of me when I express how I feel.

Beliefs such as these create a fear and avoidance of vulnerability and exploring emotions. To eradicate these negative beliefs, you can refer to the seven-step process for cognitive restructuring mentioned in Chapter 2. It may also be useful to spend time reflecting on childhood memories that trigger various emotions, ranging from happiness to rage, and allow yourself to feel those emotions once again, without minimizing or judging them.

An important message to plant in your subconscious mind is that all emotions are useful and acceptable. There are no such things as good and bad emotions, since every emotion is valuable. You can learn so much about yourself from your anger, as you can from your peace and joy. Life situations that trigger strong emotions serve a purpose, which is to help you expand your mindset and develop the skills and capabilities to grow and become a better version of yourself.

With that said, strong emotions can feel overwhelming and difficult to describe to others. It takes a lot of practice to communicate strong emotions with respect and confidence. You can start practicing communicating your emotions by following the steps mentioned below:

Label Your Emotion

Have you ever felt a strong emotion but couldn't describe it using words? You may have felt the emotion growing inside your throat, chest, or stomach becoming more intense as the triggering situation progressed. However, the lack of vocabulary to describe what you were feeling made it difficult to share the experience with your significant other.

To communicate your emotions, you need to learn how to label what you are feeling. This sounds easy; however, in practice, it can be tougher than it looks. Emotions like anger, fear, sadness, happiness, surprise, and disgust are referred to as the six primary emotions. From these six emotions, hundreds of secondary emotions are born.

It is common to mislabel emotions as one of the six primary emotions, when in fact, you are experiencing a specific secondary emotion. For example, what you believe is anger could be irritation, frustration, or rage. These secondary emotions may look similar, but they are processed and managed using different coping strategies. When you are irritated, for example, you feel a slight discomfort that can be managed by taking deep breaths and showing more patience. But when you are enraged, you are overwhelmed with anger and need to step away from the situation to regain a sense of balance.

The following chart illustrates both primary and secondary emotions. Get yourself familiar with the secondary emotions that fall under each primary emotion. If you are unfamiliar with a particular emotion, research its definition. Start to imagine the different ways secondary emotions can manifest in your relationship.

Anger	**Fear**	**Sadness**	**Happiness**	**Surprise**	**Disgust**
Irritated	Scared	Lonely	Cheerful	Excited	Resentful
Annoyed	Anxious	Tearful	Proud	Energetic	Disapproving
Frustrated	Insecure	Bored	Grateful	Amazed	Judgmental
Bitter	Threatened	Isolated	Optimistic	Shocked	Avoidant
Jealous	Rejected	Stressed	Peaceful	Aroused	Shameful
Distant	Nervous	Depressed	Satisfied	Confused	Humiliated
Hurt	Overwhelmed	Disappointed	Joyful	Startled	Awful

Connect Your Emotion to an Unfulfilled Need

Once you have identified how you are feeling, the next step is to connect your feeling to an unfulfilled need. Behind every strong emotion is a need begging to be acknowledged. For instance, if you are confused about a situation, you may need clarity. If you feel bored, you may be lacking connection.

The simple "I feel...I need..." statement can help you express your emotional experience and describe the unmet need behind it. This gives your partner enough information to empathize with what you are going through and take the necessary action. You can practice the "I feel...I need..." statement by selecting a few emotions from the chart above and matching them with appropriate needs. Here are some examples:

- I feel distant. I need more quality time with you.
- I feel insecure. I need more reassurance.
- I feel excited. I need to celebrate.

Make Requests

Showing accountability for your emotions allows your partner to listen and empathize with what you have to say, without feeling attacked or defensive. You can show accountability by using the "I feel...I need..." statement whenever you are sharing your emotions. Additionally, you can make requests on how your partner can help you respond to your needs.

Think of a way that your partner can respond to an unfulfilled need and present your request to them. Make sure that your request is simple, realistic, and within their capacity to fulfill. The easier you make the action, the less resistance they will put up. Remember to also communicate the request in a kind and respectful way, leaving enough room for your partner to say no or ask for a compromise.

Expanding on the examples provided above, here is how you can make requests:

- I feel distant. I need more quality time with you. Are you available for dinner tomorrow? I would love to see you.

- I feel insecure. I need more reassurance. Would you please initiate physical intimacy more often? It would make me feel desired.

- I feel excited. I need to celebrate. Can we go on an adventure together? I want to have fun with you.

Which of the three steps to communicating your emotions did you find most challenging: labeling your emotions, connecting emotions to needs, or making requests? Spend time working on the steps you need more practice in. Find a close friend to role-play with or rehearse the steps while looking into a mirror.

An Emotional Rollercoaster

Despite being equipped with the skills to communicate your emotions, there will be times in your relationship when you or your partner find it difficult to regulate your emotions. In other words, how you feel may change or fluctuate regularly, causing tension and stress in your relationship.

There are often good reasons for being emotionally dysregulated. For instance, you may be juggling a lot of responsibilities and feel hypersensitive to stress. You may have recently gone through a major life transition, such as losing a job, giving birth to a child, relocating to another city, or losing a loved one. Another cause for emotional dysregulation is living with a diagnosed or undiagnosed mental health condition like generalized anxiety disorder (GAD), PTSD, depression, or bipolar disorder.

When you or your partner go through these changes, you may find it tough to maintain harmony in your relationship. One minute both of you are smiling and enjoying each other's company, and the next minute you are on opposite sides of the house, upset and vowing never to speak to one another again.

This emotional rollercoaster can continue for months or years if it isn't acknowledged and addressed immediately. The longer it continues, the more strain it can place on your relationship. Even the strongest romantic relationships cannot survive years of extreme highs and lows, and conflict that is never resolved.

Some of the early warning signs that your relationship may be on an emotional rollercoaster are:

- **Breakdown of communication:** Communication issues occur when you avoid difficult conversations, feel scared of opening up to your partner, or allow arguments to end without resolving.

- **Trust issues:** Behaviors that cause a lack of trust include lying, hiding information from your partner, physical and emotional cheating, or continuously violating your partner's boundaries.

- **Misalignment of values and goals:** When you and your partner cannot agree on the fundamental values of your relationship or the future you imagine for yourselves as a couple or family, you may start to grow apart and experience frequent power struggles.

- **Unresolved conflict:** Sweeping arguments under the rug to maintain harmony in your relationship can eventually backfire. Unresolved conflict causes both of you to harbor strong emotions that build up over time and lead to feelings of contempt and resentment.

- **Personal insecurities:** Deep, unresolved emotional issues from the past can cause personal insecurities that make it difficult to connect and deepen intimacy with your partner. They may also promote destructive habits like projecting your feelings onto your partner, shifting blame, and other manipulative tactics.

It is important to discuss with your partner an action that both of you can take whenever you notice the warning signs of being on an emotional rollercoaster.

Regardless of which one of you is experiencing emotional dysregulation, you should tackle the problem as a team. Think of practical strategies that can help you reduce the tension and conflict in your relationship; examples include:

- seeking a third-party mediator like a therapist
- spending more quality time together to stay connected
- spending less time together to practice self-care
- creating relationship rituals and traditions to deepen your bond
- traveling on vacation together and taking time off work
- seeking a medical diagnosis for a suspected mental health condition
- creating stronger relationship boundaries and holding each other accountable
- joining support groups with other couples going through similar experiences

How you manage emotional rollercoasters in your relationship should be something that both of you can agree on and commit to; otherwise, the solutions won't bring long-lasting change and harmony.

Going through emotional rollercoasters should also be seen as a time for each of you to reflect on your mindsets, beliefs, and behaviors. Without judging yourself, consider whether you have been an understanding or difficult partner to deal with. Honestly ask yourself: *Have I made myself or the relationship a priority?* Moving forward, commit to being more open-minded and willing to adjust your behaviors for the betterment of your relationship (your partner should commit to doing the same).

Healing Together

When you encounter emotional issues in your relationship, you have the option to address them alone or with your significant other. The benefit of going through the healing process with your partner is that you can both walk out as stronger individuals and have a stronger relationship.

So, what does healing together look like? The most crucial step when healing as a couple is to identify the root issues you are dealing with as individuals, and between you. Knowing what the issues are can help you narrow your focus on specific areas and avoid being distracted by other minor relationship challenges. One way to identify the root issues is to think about the common themes of your arguments. What are some of the recurring disagreements you have?

After identifying the root issues, the next step is to decide on your desired outcomes. Envision your relationship after the healing process and make a list of positive developments that have occurred. This step requires you to tap into your imagination and visualize your version of a healthy romantic relationship. Share and compare notes with your partner, and narrow the list to outcomes that both of you have written down. These will be the mutually desired outcomes you will strive for.

Examples of desired outcomes could be:

- respect for each other's beliefs and viewpoints
- unconditional acceptance of each other
- honest and respectful communication
- positive resolutions after every argument
- kind and considerate feedback when mistakes are made
- commitment to spending more time together
- working together to solve personal and relationship problems
- commitment to personal growth for the betterment of the relationship

Once both of you have identified the root issues and mutually agreed on the desired outcomes, you can start researching and planning various interventions to enhance the healing process. These interventions don't have to be formal commitments like going to therapy. They can be rituals, habits, or standards that you wish to integrate into your relationship.

For example, if one of your root issues is a lack of respect and your desired outcome is to display unconditional acceptance for one another, a standard that you can set in your relationship is responding with empathy. Responding with empathy requires you to imagine what the other person is feeling and how they make sense of the world. It forces you to step outside your own mental model and look at reality through your partner's eyes. By doing this, you can understand their thought processes; how they are shaped by their past, and the emotional triggers that could be behind their behaviors. Empathy enables you to seek understanding rather than seeking to be right, and respond with compassion rather than with criticism.

Other standards that you can set in your relationship are to be more patient with one another and make a consistent effort to show support, affection, and respond to each other's needs. Setting these standards may not guarantee immediate change; however, you now have a new benchmark to work toward. For example, if you both agree to be patient with each other, you may show more self-restraint during arguments or bite your tongue when you feel the impulse to blur out unkind words.

Alternatively, you can opt to take a structured approach to healing and explore couples therapy. Couples therapy is a form of relationship counseling where you invite a coach or therapist to mediate conflict between you and your partner and provide information on how to tackle relationship problems. The benefit of speaking to a third party is that they offer unbiased and professional advice and can introduce you to techniques that can save your relationship. Over 97% of couples surveyed in a study released by the American Association of Marriage and Family reported an improvement in their emotional health after receiving treatment (AAMFT, 2015).

There are different types of couples therapy services and treatments to choose from, such as emotion-focused therapy (EFT), narrative therapy, the Gottman method, and Imago relationship therapy (IRT). When choosing a therapy, consider your relationship needs and root issues and whether there is a prevalence of trauma or attachment issues to be resolved. While couples therapy can be effective in healing your relationship, it doesn't work without your full commitment to the process. Before considering this option, make sure you and your partner are on the same page about what is expected from each of you during the healing process.

Chapter 4:

Sexual Symphony

True love is not a hide-and-seek game: in true love, both lovers seek each other. —Michael Bassey Johnson

Physical Intimacy Explained

In the previous chapter, we unpacked the second pillar of M.E.S.S, Emotional Health, and looked at the importance of addressing emotional baggage to build strong and intimate relationships. Both men and women have a full range of emotions that deserve to be explored and embraced in a safe and nurturing relationship, and sometimes, strong emotions like frustration or loneliness can mask deeper unmet needs that have gone unnoticed or overlooked.

We are now ready to move onto the third pillar of M.E.S.S, Sexual Health, which places a spotlight on the need for physical intimacy. We can define physical intimacy as the process of connecting to your partner on a deeper level that involves different forms of touch and intimacy.

One of the defining qualities of a romantic relationship is connecting to your partner's mind, heart, and body. No other type of relationship can achieve this level of connectedness. The lack of physical intimacy can therefore compromise the strength of your relationship and rob you of a connection that is exclusive for you and your significant other.

As a couple, it is your shared duty to respond to each other's need for physical intimacy. It is normal to have different interests, desires, and preferences when it comes to physical intimacy. That is why conversations around this topic are so necessary. The only way to satisfy your partner's need for physical intimacy is to understand what they expect and where their boundaries lie. In return, they can learn more about your expectations related to physical intimacy by asking questions and being open to providing what you need.

The first word that jumps to mind when discussing physical intimacy is sex. On a primal level, there is nothing romantic about sex. Two or more people engage in a physical activity that brings a powerful release of energy and a temporary high. Besides sexual gratification, sex is also used for reproductive purposes and maintaining good physical and mental health.

It is possible to have sex without an emotional connection. This is known as casual sex. Casual sex focuses on the personal experience of pleasure, and once the euphoria has faded away, the connection between the two individuals comes to an end. It is common to have casual sex during the early stages of a romantic relationship while you are getting to know your partner, and vice versa. All that is required to have casual sex is enough sexual attraction and chemistry.

A common mistake that couples make is to associate sex with love. Sex on its own does not cultivate true love. What makes sex feel like passionate love is an emotion called lust. We can define lust as a strong sexual urge or desire for someone. It is based on physical attraction, sexual fantasies, and sexual arousal. Lust isn't a bad emotion. It simply means that you are sexually attracted to somebody. Sometimes, lust can turn into love, but for that to happen, there needs to be an emotional connection.

People who have anxious or avoidant attachment styles, where they fear intimacy and may (or may not) have commitment issues, tend to have obsessions with people (which they believe is true love) that quickly escalate into casual sexual encounters. The feeling of lust and infatuation become heightened, and they convince themselves that they are falling in love. However, a few months down the line, when an emotional bond starts to form and there is a greater need for vulnerability, these anxious or avoidant individuals start to panic and feel caged in the relationship. Sooner or later, they may find reasons to exit the relationship or backpeddle to avoid developing intimacy.

As you can tell, anybody can have sex, but not everybody can experience physical intimacy. If you are looking to deepen your connection with your partner, your shared goal should be to cultivate true intimacy that transcends sex. There are a few components that are required to build true intimacy:

- feeling safe and secure in the relationship
- feeling accepted for who you are
- feeling comfortable to learn and explore
- being emotionally attuned to your partner
- feeling comfortable being silly and playful
- feeling confident expressing your sexual needs
- feeling comfortable saying no and drawing boundaries

You may be wondering how long it takes to develop this kind of intimacy. The truth is that there isn't a fixed timeframe. It may take some couples weeks or years to feel comfortable opening up to each other. The presence of trauma and emotional issues can delay this process; however, with a commitment to healing, you can eventually experience the level of physical intimacy that you both desire.

Sexual Connection

When most couples discuss sex, they talk about sexual interests, fantasies, and preferences. While these conversations are necessary, they don't get down to the core motivations for having sex.

Sex is a physical activity that is rooted in a psychological need. When you hear someone say, "I need sex," what they actually mean is they need something deeper than sex provides. Your motivation for having sex might be different from your partner's motivation for having sex. Getting to understand what sex means to both of you can deepen your emotional connection and make you feel a sense of pleasure from sexually satisfying each other.

Behind the physical act of sex are four psychological needs: security, self-esteem, autonomy, and connection. Below is a brief breakdown of each:

- **Security:** Having sex helps you feel secure in your relationship. You may use sex to ensure physical stability or long-lasting love (e.g. waiting until 90 days or until your wedding night to have sex because that makes you feel more confident in the durability of your relationship).

- **Self-esteem:** Having sex helps you feel significant and competent, especially among members of the same gender. You may use sex to seek emotional validation from your partner and feel desired by them. Not getting regular sex can feel the same as being rejected by your partner.

- **Autonomy:** Having sex offers you a sense of freedom and control. You may use sex to balance feelings of powerlessness in other areas of your life. Sex helps you escape the real world and get lost in a world of pleasure. Having diverse sexual experiences is important to you; otherwise, you may feel restricted, and subsequently controlled.

- **Connection:** Having sex helps you feel connected to your partner physically, mentally, emotionally, and spiritually. You may use sex to build intimacy and form a unique bond with your partner. Sex may also be an additional love language to communicate how much your partner means to you.

Discussing what sex means to both of you is the first step to strengthening your sexual connection. You will quickly realize that sex means so much more to your partner than what you think. This explains why the lack of sex can create emotional issues in your relationship. Depriving your partner of sex means they are unable to fulfill certain psychological needs.

When discussing your sexual needs, make sure you are both relaxed and free of distractions. Have a casual and non-judgmental conversation about what sex represents to both of you. Thereafter, you can share sexual fantasies, preferences, and boundaries to get a full picture of how both of you define and experience sex.

Navigating Sexual Experiences

It is important to understand that you are on a separate sexual journey from your partner. How you define, desire, and experience sex is not the same as how they might define, desire, and experience sex. Challenges may occur in your relationship when there is a lack of open communication around your sexual experiences and what you both expect and can offer to each other.

For example, crucial conversations to have with your partner center around common sexual problems in relationships, such as a mismatch of sex drives or the frequency of sex. As uncomfortable as these conversations may be, tackling them together can help you experience a healthy sex life where you are both satisfied with the sexual experiences you are having.

Consider the following examples of common sexual problems:

- **Low frequency of sex:** It is common for partners to have different expectations when it comes to the frequency of sex. This is often due to a mismatch in libido, or low sex drive. Many factors can cause low sex drive, such as chronic illness, fatigue, mental health issues, unresolved relationship conflict, or a mundane sex routine.

- **Lack of sexual pleasure:** People's bodies respond to sex differently. Some people can achieve an orgasm comparatively quicker or easier than others. Moreover, the feeling of sexual intercourse may be more pleasurable to some more than others. Conversations around sexual pleasure can help couples find different ways to sexually stimulate each other to make the experience enjoyable for both parties.

- **Loss of excitement:** In long-term relationships, it is common for sex to become mechanical and subsequently boring. Due to work responsibilities and other life stressors, couples can get stuck in the same sex routine and lose desire for each other. Reigniting the spark requires curiosity and openness to try new experiences and being playful with one another.

- **Lack of initiation:** Partners, more typically men, sometimes grow tired of being the only person to initiate sex. What's surprising is that many times the expectation to share this responsibility is often not communicated. In other words, women are unaware that their partners would like them to initiate sex more frequently. Communicating this need can ensure both partners feel desired and understood.

- **Managing life transitions:** When couples go through changes in their relationships, such as working longer hours, starting a family, grieving the loss of a loved one, or moving in with aging parents, their sex life can become less of a priority. Managing and communicating expectations is crucial during these periods of your relationship, as well as exploring other forms of intimacy outside the bedroom to stay connected.

It is not easy to bring up any of the problems mentioned above because the last thing you want is to upset your partner. However, consider the fact that behind your desire for sex are important psychological needs. Discussing sexual problems helps you express concerns, listen and empathize with your partner's needs, and work toward finding solutions that are suitable for both of you. Even though your sexual journeys are different, you can only achieve a great sex life when you negotiate expectations and create a synchronized sexual experience.

There are a few tips to remember when having conversations about sexual needs and challenges:

- **Choose the right timing:** Bring up the subject of sexual needs or challenges when both of you are in a private setting, preferably sober and in a calm state of mind. Avoid the subject during times when either of you are stressed, distracted, or going through emotional issues.

- **Be direct but non-judgmental:** Share your views without sounding critical or judgmental of your partner. Be willing to listen and empathize with your partner's perspective, rather than insisting on your viewpoint. Remember that the best outcome is when you both walk away feeling accepted, respected, and understood. Focus on things you can both agree on and expand on them.

- **Offer positive reinforcement:** Sex is a sensitive topic that can affect how your partner views himself or herself. Be extremely careful when expressing your thoughts and feelings to avoid making your partner feel inadequate, unattractive, or undesirable. For every concern you bring up, mention three to five things that you admire about your partner. Emphasize the point that they are not the problem, the situation is.

- **Bring solutions to the table:** Whenever you bring up sexual concerns or challenges, follow up with practical solutions that both of you can try. This relieves a lot of pressure from your partner and shows your willingness to cooperate in enhancing your sex life. Research different methods and treatments to solve your problems, including seeking professional medical advice if needed.

If you are afraid of initiating conversations around sex with your partner, consider seeking a third-party mediator like a couple's therapist or sex coach to help you navigate the issues you are facing in your relationship.

Intimacy Beyond the Bedroom

While sex is a major component of physical intimacy, it isn't the only way that couples can stay physically connected. Intimacy can be defined as a feeling of closeness between two people that enables them to show up vulnerable and authentic to each other. This means that any activity that promotes closeness between couples can increase physical intimacy.

The reason why couples need to consider intimacy beyond the bedroom is that a long-lasting romantic relationship cannot be sustained by sex alone. There will be seasons during your relationship when you are unable to have sex as often as you would like, and you are required to find other ways to maintain an emotional connection with your loved one.

The absence of sex in your relationship shouldn't be the "make-or-break" factor; however, this doesn't mean that having a sexless relationship is acceptable either. The main point is that during gaps of not having sex in your relationship, there should be other ways of maintaining closeness with your partner.

Familiarizing yourself with the building blocks of intimacy can help you gain a better understanding of how to build intimacy outside the bedroom. The building blocks of intimacy are:

Warmth

Warmth is the ability to lower your psychological defenses and invite your partner into your physical and emotional space. The objective is to make them feel welcomed in your presence and comfortable to be themselves. You can show warmth to your partner by approaching situations with a light and understanding attitude and treating your partner like you would a close friend.

Confidentiality

Confidentiality is a spoken agreement that you make with your partner to protect their right to privacy and always act in their best interest. What your partner shares with you or how they express themselves in front of you is kept private. It may take time before your partner feels emotionally safe to confide in you. Meanwhile, you can show them that you can be trusted by respecting their right to privacy and other boundaries.

Vulnerability

Vulnerability is the ability to be sensitive around your partner without feeling exposed or judged. Whenever you are with them, you feel comfortable being uncensored and sharing thoughts that you wouldn't otherwise share with people, such as your childhood memories, dreams and ambitions, or sexual needs and fantasies. Since showing vulnerability is an emotional risk, focus on creating an emotionally safe and validating space for your partner to freely be themselves.

Authenticity

Authenticity is being unapologetic about who you are and feeling safe to be yourself in front of others. There are certain relationships where authenticity may be inappropriate, such as new friendships or work relationships. But within loving romantic relationships, authenticity is celebrated. Unfortunately, authenticity isn't something that you can force out of your partner, but giving them regular reassurance can encourage them to let down their guard.

Closeness

Closeness is the feeling of being seen and accepted by your partner. This feeling creates a strong bond between you that cannot be broken by distance, silence, or the normal ups and downs of relationships. Closeness can be built through open heartfelt conversations, intentional physical touch, playfulness, and being vulnerable with each other.

The five components of intimacy mentioned can help you develop emotional intimacy, which is a sacred emotional bond between you and your partner that isn't built or sustained by sex, but only by warmth, confidentiality, vulnerability, authenticity, and closeness. An elevated version of emotional intimacy is spiritual intimacy, which is a sacred bond that forms when you connect over shared values and beliefs (more information about how to achieve this coming in the next chapter).

If you are interested in exploring intimacy outside the bedroom, there are some bonding tips you can try:

- **Show interest in your partner's hobbies or passions.** Develop closeness with your partner by trying to immerse yourself in their world (while respecting their boundaries). Get to know more about their hobbies and passions, and why they matter. You can even watch or participate in their hobbies to create core memories.

- **Listen, observe, and adjust.** You can learn a lot about your partner by listening attentively when they speak and observing their behaviors. This is a form of empathy that helps you adjust how you interact with your partner based on who they are and how they desire to be loved.

- **Spend quiet time together.** Shared silences can be a great way to connect on an emotional and spiritual level. They encourage you to be yourself around your partner and overcome the fear of rejection. Shared silences can also encourage self-care and individuality without the need to spend time apart from your loved one.

- **Have more shared experiences.** Making memories with your partner adds excitement and playfulness to your relationship. A strong connection is built and maintained by going on adventures and taking risks together. Through shared experiences, you can learn new things about your partner and get to see them in a relaxed and low-stress environment.

Overcoming Sexual Trauma and Fear

A critical aspect of improving your sex life is addressing past sexual trauma and fears that might cause you or your partner to avoid sex or intimacy. Experiencing sexual abuse or assault affects your physical, mental, and emotional well-being, and can change your perspective about relationships. With the proper treatment, you can address some of these issues, but the toughest barrier to overcome is learning to feel safe and trusting of others again.

Due to the trauma of having your physical boundaries violated and being placed in a life-threatening situation, romantic relationships may no longer feel like safe spaces to express who you are and show vulnerability. Instead, relationships may become the source of anxiety and many of your insecurities.

For instance, as much as you desire to connect with someone on a deep level, you may doubt whether the attraction is mutual, whether or not the relationship will end in rejection, or whether the connection is based on true love or some kind of dependency. These fears and doubts could result in self-sabotaging behaviors like disappearing after sexual encounters, displaying commitment issues, or refusing to be open about your feelings.

A couple once came into my counseling room with a problem related to this. The young lady was a survivor of sexual abuse at the hands of her ex-partner, which made it difficult for her to form an emotional connection with her current partner. To deal with the trauma, and protect herself from facing a similar betrayal again, she decided to completely block out her feelings. This became an issue in her current relationship, since her partner desired to build a stronger connection beyond sex.

By recognizing that she was emotionally unavailable to her partner, she was able to make an effort to let down her guard. They both decided to take a few months off sex to establish emotional intimacy. During this time, they focused on spending quality time together, having meaningful conversations, and connecting on their shared beliefs and values. When they eventually got back to having sex, the couple reported feeling closer and emotionally invested in their relationship.

Sexual trauma affects your ability to lower your defenses in a relationship and trust the process of getting to know someone and falling in love. By understanding how your past traumatic experiences have impacted your ability to connect with others, you can be mindful of avoidant, dismissive, and self-sabotaging behaviors that compromise your relationship.

If you are a survivor of sexual abuse and assault, there are ways to slowly rebuild your sense of trust and safety in romantic relationships, such as:

- **Know your emotional triggers.** Get into the habit of identifying and writing down your emotional triggers. These can be words, phrases, actions, people, or places that activate your stress response. Discuss your triggers with your partner and offer alternative, non-triggering behaviors they can practice.

- **Set boundaries.** Be clear about your physical, mental, and emotional limits by setting appropriate boundaries. Your focus should be on reducing interactions that make you feel unsafe, such as certain kinds of physical touch, specific tone of voice or language, or topics you are not ready to explore.

- **Reconnect with yourself.** The relationship with your partner is a mirror of the relationship with yourself. If you want to show up as an open, warm, and empathetic partner, practice displaying those traits toward yourself. Treat yourself like you would somebody you care for deeply. Schedule time for self-care, journaling, and hobbies you enjoy.

- **Find a therapist.** Sexual trauma can create deep issues that require a therapist to address. Therapy is an effective way to confront and heal trauma, even decades after the event or period of your life took place. If you are ready to take this step, look for a therapist with experience working with survivors of abuse.

If you are dating or married to someone who is a survivor of sexual abuse and assault, there are ways to connect and communicate your desire to support them. These may include:

- **Educate yourself on the impact of sexual trauma.** Get a better understanding of what your partner is going through by learning about sexual abuse and its impact on the survivor and their close relationships.

- **Be sensitive toward your partner's triggers.** It is better to ask questions and seek clarity about what triggers your partner than to learn after the fact. You can also ask for guidance on how to adjust your behaviors to make them feel comfortable.

- **Be willing to explore intimacy outside of sex.** If your partner wants to wait before getting intimate, find other ways to strengthen your connection that don't involve sex. You can also discuss other forms of physical touch, like cuddling and kissing, which your partner may be open to.

- **Hold your partner accountable.** It is not your responsibility to fix or rescue your partner. You are supposed to play a supportive role to offer encouragement when they need it. However, the natural give-and-take that occurs between partners should remain an expectation. When your partner stops showing affection and support toward you, it is necessary to hold them accountable.

Chapter 5:

Spiritual Bond

You can never love another person unless you are equally involved in the beautiful but difficult spiritual work of learning to love yourself. —John O'Donohue

Soulful Synergy

In the previous chapter, we discussed the third pillar of M.E.S.S, Sexual Health, and looked at the value of sex and intimacy in strengthening the bond between couples. We discovered that sex is essential for healthy relationships because behind the motivation for having sex are four vital psychological needs to be fulfilled. However, physical intimacy goes beyond the bedroom and can include couple activities that promote warmth, authenticity, vulnerability, closeness, and confidentiality.

We can now explore M.E.S.S's fourth and final pillar, Spiritual Health. Spiritual health is achieved by physical, mental, and emotional alignment. It is characterized by feeling good about yourself, inside and out. Being grounded in nature or connected to a higher power or purpose can help you achieve alignment.

There isn't a right or wrong way to practice spirituality. For example, some people might go the religious route, while others might go the self-healing or altruistic route. Whether you are a member of a church or hike mountains religiously, the most important aspect of spiritual health is establishing a deeper connection to yourself and those around you.

Spiritual intimacy, a concept we touched on earlier, is the sacred bond that forms when you connect with your significant other over shared values and beliefs. It is difficult to develop this type of intimacy without first establishing a strong emotional connection. Your beliefs, values, and life's purpose are some of the core attributes that form the structure of your life. It is easier to bond over shared history, emotional needs, or lifestyle expectations than to present your core beliefs and values to each other.

If you find that your partner is hesitant to open up about their beliefs and values, it is because of how much courage and vulnerability it takes to speak about these topics. They may care about you deeply but prefer to continue getting to know you before revealing their fundamental principles.

Spiritual Compatibility vs. Spiritual Incompatibility

Spiritual intimacy is not mandatory when entering a romantic relationship. However, as you get to know each other and consider a future together, you will need to know whether you are spiritually compatible or not. Being spiritually compatible doesn't necessarily mean sharing the same religious views or showing interest in the same spiritual practices. It is about being able to maintain closeness and mutual respect as both of you grow and exercise your beliefs and values.

Spiritual incompatibility occurs when one or both of you cannot look past your differences to the extent of limiting your growth potential. In other words, you may expect your partner to adopt your beliefs and values or place restrictions on how they can and cannot express themselves. By doing this, you become a barrier to his or her personal growth, and this can lead to resentment. Being in a relationship with a partner who has different ideas on spirituality can be a dealbreaker if you are unwilling to learn from them and allow them to grow in their beliefs.

I remember working with a couple who was preparing to get married. A few sessions into our meetings, we landed on the subject of spirituality. At first, both of them seemed to be on the same page, until they started to describe their ideal spiritual practices once they were married. The lady who had conservative views about spirituality described going to church, honoring religious holidays, and having Bible readings around the breakfast table.

The gentleman who had liberal views and did not belong to any particular religion described spending silent moments with his spouse and taking afternoon walks to get fresh air. Their interpretations of spirituality were not the problem, the lady's lack of acceptance of her fiancé's outlook on spirituality was. She challenged his understanding of spirituality and tried to convince him to accept her views.

Being a liberal person, he could see merits in her argument, but didn't feel as strongly about following religious traditions. Once again, she attempted to prove why he was wrong and her method was right. After a few rounds of back-and-forth, it was clear to see that this couple, although madly in love with each other, were spiritually incompatible.

You don't have to wait until pre-marital counseling to discover whether you and your partner are spiritually compatible or incompatible. For instance, spiritually compatible partners typically demonstrate the following qualities:

- You feel alive and energized when you are in their presence.

- You have evidence of your partner making a positive impact on your life.

- Other relationships in your life have improved as a result of being with your partner.

- You are inspired to grow and pursue your goals due to the influence of your partner.

- You have a deep feeling of loyalty to your partner.

- You are not afraid of expressing your love, even if it causes you to step outside your comfort zone.

- You find ways to stay connected to your partner, even when they are physically away.

- You have a sixth sense of what your partner feels and what they need.

- When your partner is upset, your mood quickly changes too.

- You telepathically communicate with each other through thoughts, feelings, signs, and symbols.

Spiritually compatible couples have deep soul ties that are formed long before the individuals meet. Their first encounter with each other feels like a reunion of some sort because of how connected and comfortable they are with one another. If you believe in the concept of soulmates, your spiritually compatible partner can be considered one. The bond you share feels like it has been built over a lifetime and prepared for such a time as this.

In contrast, if you are not spiritually compatible with your partner, you will notice the following signs:

- You care for each other, but often fight over trivial matters.

- Certain qualities about your partner irritate you.

- You feel tired or drained when you are in their presence.
- Your life has felt bland, difficult, or cursed since being with your partner.
- You have been together for several months or years, but the relationship hasn't progressed.
- Your physical and mental health has declined since being with your partner.
- You have thoughts or fantasies about cheating on your partner.
- You don't feel enthusiastic about the future of your relationship.
- You have become cynical about relationships since being with your partner.
- You procrastinate working on your goals and following through with tasks.

As mentioned before, spiritual intimacy goes together with emotional intimacy. If there is a lack of emotional connection in your relationship, you will likely be spiritually incompatible. Make an effort to deepen the emotional bond between you to improve your spiritual connectedness.

Finding Common Ground

Being spiritually incompatible is not a relationship dealbreaker if you are both willing to meet each other halfway and find common ground. As already mentioned, it is expected for individuals to enter romantic relationships with different beliefs, especially now that we live in secular societies where diverse ideas and beliefs are accepted. How you both manage your differences is what makes or breaks your relationship.

Finding common ground is about looking for things you can agree about and making those factors your sole focus. Neither of you is forced to give up your personal views or make extreme compromises. You simply need to find areas where your interests, beliefs, and values overlap and place less emphasis on areas where you might disagree.

When seeking to find common ground on spiritual matters, open and honest discussions about your personal views are important. Treat these discussions as exploration exercises to gather as much information about your partner's beliefs as you can, and vice versa. Encourage taking down notes, asking clarifying questions, and making an effort to understand where they are coming from.

Empathy is a crucial skill when learning to find common ground. You don't need to agree with your partner to appreciate their outlook on life. Empathy forces you to dig deep and figure out why your partner thinks the way they do and how their personal history has shaped their fears, desires, and hopes for the future.

Finding common ground is also about addressing the elephant in the room and creating transparency between you. Find the time to tackle those controversial topics in your relationship and acknowledge where both of you stand on the matter. Once again, the goal is not to convince each other of who's right and who's wrong, but rather to seek clarity and let go of assumptions.

For example, you may be aware that your partner is not enthusiastic about starting a family, whereas you are a family-orientated person and strongly desire to start a family one day. Instead of avoiding the topic of family, spend time understanding each other's views and what informs them. If there are questions that you have about this topic, pose them to your partner and give them a chance to respond in their own words. Through open conversations, you could potentially find common ground or discover that you may not be the right partner for each other.

A fun exercise that you can practice with your partner is taking turns to share your thoughts on core values. On a set of flashcards, write down common values with a bold black marker. Examples of values include:

- truth
- honesty
- religion
- family
- loyalty

- love
- generosity
- peace
- accountability
- gratitude
- leadership
- teamwork
- respect
- physical intimacy
- quality time
- adventure

Strike a balance between sharing your thoughts and listening to your partner share theirs. The goal of this exercise is to find common ground, so you need to pay careful attention to what your partner says to find overlapping ideas, interests, and opinions. Practice this exercise every few months to assess if you are still on the same page about some values, or whether there have been shifts in your perspectives.

Unseen Connection

What makes a spiritual connection different from an emotional connection is that it can develop and become stronger without exchanging words with your partner. For instance, your partner doesn't have to express their emotions for you to sense what they are feeling.

One of the often overlooked strategies for deepening a spiritual connection is non-verbal communication. With non-verbal communication, messages are passed between individuals through body language, facial expressions, and physical presence. Think about what a warm hug or loving eye contact communicates to your partner. For some people, actions carry a stronger message than a few words.

Researchers predict that 90% of all communication is non-verbal (Hickman, 2020). This means when you learn to master non-verbal communication, you can control 90% of messages passed to your significant other. As a result, you can reduce misunderstandings and intentionally express your love.

There are common types of non-verbal communication that couples perform, such as:

- smiling
- eye contact

- pat on the back
- hugs and cuddling
- showing sympathy
- sitting close to one another
- respecting personal space
- loving and respectful tone of voice
- facing each other during conversations
- wearing a pleasant perfume or cologne
- making an effort to dress well and be presentable for your partner

In this section, we are going to explore the power of shared silence in deepening a spiritual connection. In relationships, there are two types of silences, one being destructive and the other being beneficial. You may be familiar with the concept of silent treatment, a destructive silence where one person refuses to talk as a tactic to gain more control of the situation. When the silent treatment is given, the lines of communication are closed and the victim feels emotionally invalidated.

However, there is another type of silence known as positive silence, where a couple agrees to take a break from talking, but maintains a connection by being in each other's presence. The lines of communication remain open by creating emotional safety so that both individuals can freely be themselves without feeling awkward. Imagine doing what you would normally do alone but in the company of your partner. This is what positive silence entails.

You may also be interested in turning positive silence into a relationship ritual. For example, once a day or week, you can schedule a silent activity to perform with your partner. This could be as simple as taking a shower together, silently praying with each other, taking late afternoon walks, or visiting a bookstore together. You don't need to place strict rules to not talk at all. Some conversation here and there is perfectly fine. What's important is getting comfortable being in the presence of your partner without needing to entertain each other.

Your Spiritual Walk

Understandably, spiritual health isn't something that you consciously think about every day. Thus, to prioritize growth in this area of your relationship, it can be helpful to develop a spiritual practice. In simple terms, a spiritual practice is a spiritual activity that becomes a consistent part of your life. How frequently you perform the practice is up to you. For example, going to church is a spiritual practice that occurs on Sundays mostly; meditation is a spiritual practice that can be performed once or twice a day.

To build spiritual intimacy, you can identify spiritual practices to perform as a couple. These can be daily or weekly rituals that help you connect beyond the physical, mental, and emotional levels. Couples who adopt spiritual practices tend to have lower stress and anxiety levels. This happens as a result of improved communication and self-awareness. Another positive benefit of developing spiritual practices is being able to learn and practice healthy relationship habits, like spending quality time together, being a good listener, and showing greater vulnerability.

Engaging in spiritual practices with your partner can be a lot of fun, especially when spiritual growth is a personal goal for both of you. Why travel on the spiritual path alone when you can do it with your partner beside you?

Before you pick spiritual practices to try, take a moment to sit down with your partner and answer the following questions as honestly as you can. Remember to find common ground when you discover areas of disagreement.

1. What are our intentions for adopting a spiritual practice?

____

____

2. What are we willing to explore?

3. What are we **not** willing to explore?

4. How much time can we realistically devote to a practice, in a week?

5. Do mornings or evenings work better for us?

6. Do indoor or outdoor activities work better for us?

7. Who can we consult if we need information?

After responding to these questions, you will have a better idea of what types of spiritual practices will be suitable to explore as a couple. Remember, you are welcome to engage in solo practices to deepen your personal spiritual life.

A few suggestions on activities to try with your partner include:

- Pray together.
- Practice silent meditation.
- Set positive intentions daily.
- Find a hobby you can practice.
- Plan and review goals and milestones.
- Have weekly gratitude sessions.
- Create a morning and bedtime routine.
- Recite positive affirmations to each other.
- Respond to your partner in their love languages.
- Volunteer or support a local cause as a couple.
- Spend meal time together (at least once a day).

Healing Together

Forgiveness is another spiritual practice that can bring couples together and enhance their spiritual connection. This practice is taught by various religions and encouraged by coaches, therapists, and spiritual teachers. Everyone may not always agree on beliefs and values, but what most people can agree on is the benefit of practicing forgiveness.

Forgiveness is the choice to settle wrongdoings that have been committed by others, so you can give yourself closure and heal. The true process of forgiveness occurs after you have made this choice, and can take months and sometimes years to complete (i.e. fully heal from the wound).

Couples hurt each other all the time, yet rarely does the offender admit wrongdoing or the victim practice forgiveness. Instead, they play a game of keeping scores with one another and weaponize the mistakes their partner makes during arguments. For example, how many times have you heard the following phrases during a conflict with your partner?

- You always do this...
- But remember what you did to me?
- Don't forget about the incident last month...
- Don't act innocent.
- I'm not listening? What about you?
- Don't make me bring up the past!

These phrases reveal two things—a lack of accountability and forgiveness. Without accountability and forgiveness, you may find it difficult to repair your relationship after arguments. Each fight lays another brick of resentment until eventually, you grow apart.

Practicing forgiveness is not a favor that you do for your "undeserving" partner. It is a form of self-care that enables you to move past painful situations and release strong emotions like anger, betrayal, rejection, and disappointment. Forgiveness helps you take your power back and refuse to allow another person's actions to define who you are or change the way you think and feel.

The process of forgiveness can be uncomfortable. Not only do you need to process strong emotions triggered by the offense, but you also need to find it in your heart to empathize with your partner. You might ask yourself: *How can I empathize with them without justifying what they have done to me?*

The fact of the matter is that you were hurt by their actions, not by them as an individual. Learning how to separate them from their behaviors can help you seek to understand what compelled them to act in a certain way. Perhaps they are living with a diagnosed or undiagnosed mental illness, recently suffered the loss of a loved one, or have unprocessed emotional baggage. Looking at the situation from this perspective will make it easier to reach a place of forgiveness without necessarily condoning their behaviors.

Another challenge of practicing forgiveness is convincing your brain that the offense happened in the past and should be left in the past. For instance, your partner may have lied to you about an important issue a year ago, but that doesn't mean they are likely to respond the same way when presented with similar circumstances. This type of faulty thinking is a cognitive distortion known as generalization. When you generalize, you assume that what has happened before will likely happen in the future.

When you choose to forgive your partner, you also choose to accept reality for what it is. In other words, what happened yesterday is not the same as what is happening right now. Holding onto the past out of fear of being hurt again will only cause stress and suffering in the present moment. Furthermore, holding onto the past makes you powerless to control what is happening (or can happen) at this moment.

Imagine forgiveness to be the same as opening your hands in anticipation of receiving new experiences in your relationship, and unforgiveness as clenching your fists. Walking around with your fists clenched means that you are unable to receive both pleasant and unpleasant experiences from your partner. Even though you are safe from getting hurt again, the relationship reaches a dead-end and can no longer positively impact your life.

The Four Steps of Forgiveness

Making forgiveness one of your spiritual practices can help you live according to your values and maintain a certain standard in your relationship. For example, if you value peace, forgiveness helps you restore harmony in your relationship after arguments. If you value teamwork, forgiveness helps you work together with your partner to find solutions for recurring relationship problems.

Another spiritual benefit of practicing forgiveness is that you can process emotional triggers and painful situations as they arise, and immediately accept and let go. This prevents you from harboring strong emotions or developing psychological issues over time. It is good spiritual hygiene to maintain physical, mental, and emotional alignment. However, this can only be achieved when you are free from physical or emotional blockages caused by unforgiveness.

If you are prepared to choose forgiveness, the following steps can help you get started:

Step 1: Acknowledge Your Hurt Feelings

The first step is to acknowledge that you have been hurt and identify what the hurt feels like. Identify the emotional impact your partner's actions have had on you. Consider what feelings you are experiencing as a result of your partner's actions. For example, being cheated on by your partner makes you feel angry, small, and insecure, or being name-called robs you of respect and being treated with dignity.

Step 2: Separate the Actions From the Person

Make a distinction in your mind between your partner's poor choice of behavior and who they are as a person. Painting your partner out to be a monster makes you feel good for a short while, but prevents you from confronting the real issue, which is how they treated you.

The truth of the matter is that your partner is not a bad person, they simply behaved badly. You don't have to demonize your partner to heal from what happened. Healing begins with acceptance of the truth, and this occurs when you can focus on the actions and how they may have violated your values or boundaries. Remind yourself about why you cannot tolerate such actions from your partner, or anybody else.

Step 3: Manage Your Ego

If you feel a sense of inner resistance whenever you think about the offense, it could be your ego battling inside of you, resisting the healing process. Your ego always wants to feel in control of your life circumstances, and being hurt by someone you care about is interpreted by your ego as being in a life-threatening situation. Managing your ego refers to being mindful of your tendencies to go back and forth between forgiving and being closed off to the process, or the urge to lash out at your partner and project your feelings.

Step 4: Be Patient With Yourself

The words "I forgive you" are uttered instantly, but the process of forgiveness takes time. Don't expect to return to your normal self or rebuild intimacy soon after forgiving your partner. It takes time to accept what happened, process your emotions, and restore trust in the relationship. Show compassion toward yourself by not rushing the process or forcing yourself to return to old routines and habits. Ask your partner to be patient and understanding of your journey as well.

These four steps don't happen over a weekend, they can happen over months and years. To truly get the most out of the practice of forgiveness, forget about timelines and focus on letting go of the past and accepting reality for what it is.

Chapter 6:

The Bridge Over the M.E.S.S

Communication leads to community, that is, to understanding, intimacy, and mutual valuing. —Rollo May

Love's Language

The previous chapter discussed the fourth and final pillar of M.E.S.S, Spiritual Health. We looked at ways to become spiritually compatible with your partner, such as finding common ground, connecting on shared values, sharing silences, and developing spiritual practices. This concludes our in-depth examination of the four pillars. The remaining chapters focus on offering practical strategies for cleaning up the M.E.S.S in your relationship and putting these pillars into action.

The first strategy we are going to explore is open communication. This refers to the ability to share thoughts and emotions clearly and compassionately. Most couples know how to talk at each other, but not how to speak to each other. As a result, communication tends to feel combative, and the core intention of the message is lost in translation.

Open communication challenges you to communicate with empathy and respect for your partner, seeking to understand more than you attempt to be understood. To do this, you are encouraged to start thinking in terms of "we" and "us" instead of "I" and "me." Every thought and emotion you communicate should be packaged in a way that makes it easier for your partner to receive. This doesn't mean that you need to change the content of your message; you simply need to be mindful of your delivery. As the famous saying goes, "It's not what you say, but how you say it."

Learning how to speak your partner's verbal and non-verbal love languages is essential when addressing issues related to M.E.S.S. For example, when your partner fails to respond to one of your emotional needs, how you communicate your concerns can either make them defensive or enthusiastic about adjusting their behaviors. Your partner may be easily triggered by yelling, a critical tone of voice, or the use of manipulative language. Therefore, your message should be mindful of these triggers and carefully crafted to achieve the best outcomes.

Something else to consider is that your partner's verbal and non-verbal love languages may be different from yours. Many years ago, I remember working with a couple with communication issues where the man and woman had opposite love languages. The man preferred logical results-based communication with a clear objective guiding the conversation. If they were planning to go out on a date, he only wanted to know the date, time, and venue. If his partner was upset, he would go straight into problem-solving mode without wanting to find out the details.

The woman, on the other hand, preferred abstract emotions-based communication where ideas could be explored and examined. Whenever she would share her thoughts and feelings, she would bring elements of the past, present, and future, and incorporate psychology, philosophy, and anything else she could think of at that moment. Due to the free-spirited nature of her communication style, she often felt rushed, ignored, and misunderstood by her partner. She enjoyed talking for the sake of talking, while for him, talking was unnecessary if it didn't serve a purpose.

Over some therapy sessions, they learned how to become masters at communicating each other's love languages and striking a good balance between their individual communication needs. The man learned how to ask a few open-ended questions to make conversations interesting and stimulating for his partner. The woman learned to summarize her messages, keeping them short and impactful. In the end, they were able to combine their love languages and create a new language that fulfilled both of their needs.

Perfecting Your Delivery

A healthy romantic relationship is not built on praise and recognition alone. There will be times when you have to sit down with your partner and have tough conversations that can help you grow closer. You might fear upsetting your partner by bringing up sensitive topics around mental, emotional, sexual, or spiritual needs. However, remember that it is rarely the content of your message that triggers others, but how you deliver the message. Working on your delivery can ensure that you communicate clearly with as few misunderstandings as possible.

One of the habits to be mindful of when communicating with your partner is being defensive. A few physiological changes will occur when you step into defensive mode, such as the loss of concentration and hearing, tingling or numbness, sweating, hot flushes, muscle tension, and tightness of the chest, to name a few.

Communicating in a defensive state is never a good idea because your capacity to listen and empathize with your partner is compromised. For example, when your partner approaches you with needs, concerns, or feedback, be careful not to respond with judgmental, accusatory, or dismissive language, which sounds like this:

- You never listen to me.
- Don't make me get angry.
- You don't know what you're talking about.
- So, who cares?
- Look, I said what I said. Take it or leave it.

- I'm not the problem, you are.

It is worth repeating that no constructive conversation can take place in a defensive climate. With tensions running high and both of you feeling attacked or misunderstood, you are likely to cause each other a lot of pain.

The solution to defensive communication is to create a supportive environment where you lead with curiosity, acceptance, and a mindset to learn from your partner. To do this, both of you must be in a calm state of mind, have stabilized moods, and be free of distractions. If you are at home, find a quiet corner or room where you can have a private conversation.

When showing support to your partner, there are three communication rules to remember:

Describe, Don't Judge

Whenever you are expressing your ideas and opinions, always assume that you don't know all the facts. Avoid making sweeping judgments or negative assumptions about what you are hearing. It is always best to focus on sharing your experience by describing what you think or feel and leaving room for your partner to provide clarity or expand on their message.

Example: When you say, "I don't care," it makes me think that you don't care about me. Is that what you mean?

Look for Solutions, Not Problems

Have you noticed how bringing up an issue during a conversation can lead to another issue being raised, until the matter snowballs and becomes bigger than what you had expected? To prevent an avalanche of problems from being put on the table, focus on discussing one issue during one conversation, and guiding your partner toward finding solutions.

Example: I hear that you would like me to show more affection. Can you help me understand what that might look like?

Show Respect Before Demanding Respect

Showing your partner respect, even when you cannot seem to agree on an issue, makes them feel seen, heard, and accepted. How you desire to be respected may look different from how your partner desires to be respected. For instance, they may be sensitive to the volume and tone of your voice, dismissive body language, or using unkind words and language. Respect communicates acceptance, and this is something that both men and women need. However, before you can demand respect, you have to set an example by showing respect.

Example: We may disagree on this issue, but I understand where you are coming from, and thank you for sharing your thoughts with me.

Adapt Your Communication Style

If you have been together for longer than three months, you would have picked up on the ways your partner processes and responds to situations. For instance, you may have noticed tendencies like using jokes to ease tension or insisting nothing is wrong when they look visibly upset.

By observing your partner's behaviors, you can also identify their predominant communication style, which is the standard method they use to convey messages. Your partner's communication style was not adopted overnight; it is a pattern that has formed over many decades and has been reinforced by their beliefs, mindset, and habits. This means that you cannot change your partner's communication style by forcing them to learn new communication skills. This pattern is ingrained in their subconscious mind and can take years of therapy to replace.

Instead of seeking to change how your partner conveys messages, you can take a proactive approach and learn how to adapt your message to their predominant communication style (and vice versa). Below is an outline of the four communication styles and tips on how to adapt your messages accordingly.

Passive

A passive communicator conceals their motives and true intentions when sharing thoughts and feelings. They tend to speak in circles, riddles, or present both sides of an argument but never come to a definitive conclusion. In a relationship, a passive communicator can come across as a people-pleaser. They would rather hide their true feelings or compromise their boundaries than be forced to confront their partner and risk upsetting them.

Solutions: Help your partner express their views by asking direct questions to get a yes or no answer. When they share ideas or opinions, offer validation to show respect. While their passivity can be frustrating sometimes, avoid putting them in high-stakes one-on-one situations. Be calm and collected around them, and create a comfortable environment where they can open up if they choose to.

Passive-Aggressive

A passive-aggressive communicator appears non-threatening but operates from a place of anger and retaliation. The deceptive front they put up is intentionally created to hide their dark motivations. In a relationship, a passive-aggressive communicator finds subtle ways to express their disapproval instead of openly sharing their emotions. As a result, their words often don't match their actions. It can be difficult to know where you stand with them because what they need from you is not obvious.

Solutions: Your partner may have a deep-rooted fear of rejection or abandonment, which makes them afraid of voicing their true feelings. Practice being empathetic and non-judgmental when communicating with them. Avoid showing any verbal or non-verbal signs of disapproval like rolling your eyes, sighing, looking away, folding your arms, or responding with sarcasm or interrogative questions.

Aggressive

An aggressive communicator has an intimidating aura or physical stance that creates a hostile communicative environment. They often go into conversations closed-minded and prepared for a debate or argument. In a relationship, an aggressive communicator's objective is to control the conversation and come out on top. Whenever they feel challenged, they will raise their voice, use hurtful language, interrupt you while you speak, and share their opinions in a blunt and inconsiderate way.

Solutions: Your partner is naturally in defensive mode and struggles to listen and empathize with what you have to say. The aim is to get them to relax and lower their guard. Gently remind them that you are on the same team and working together to solve problems. Set communication rules before addressing issues and hold each other accountable. Reassure them that you understand where they are coming from and appreciate their contributions.

Assertive

An assertive communicator is confident and has a high level of self-awareness and emotional intelligence. They can identify and describe what they are feeling, and at the same time, put themselves in someone else's shoes. In a relationship, an assertive communicator works toward win-win situations. They are willing to listen as much as they speak and make compromises to find common ground. Their straightforward, no-nonsense approach to conflict resolution can sometimes make them come across as aggressive; however, this is their method of getting to the root of issues so they can deal with facts rather than being distracted by emotions.

Solutions: Your partner is willing to take ownership of their mistakes and work toward solving conflict. Interact with them by asking for their opinion or seeking solutions. Show them that you are a team player by taking your share of responsibility and being committed to mutually beneficial outcomes.

Listening to Understand

Over the years, I have found that the majority of communication issues faced by couples have to do with the lack of listening, whether it is intentional or unintentional. Wherever there is a lack of listening, there is also a lack of understanding.

What many people call listening is simply looking in their partner's direction and nodding at the right moments. No real effort is put into paying attention, processing the information, and reflecting on the message. Sometimes, the lack of listening is a coping mechanism that others might turn to when they are feeling overwhelmed. Earlier on, we spoke about the destructive type of silence called the silent treatment, which is characterized by a lack of listening.

Responding to stressful situations by refusing to listen doesn't make the situations better. When you are completely shut off from your partner, the conflict continues indefinitely without reaching a peaceful resolution. I have always given my clients advice to use conflict and disagreements in their relationships as an opportunity to listen more attentively. This is when they should pay the most attention to what their significant others have to say, so they can squash the beef before it gets any bigger.

Two types of listening skills can improve the quality of communication in your relationship. The first is known as active listening, which is the ability to direct your focus on the speaker and the message they are sharing. The goal of active listening is to observe and understand what is being communicated verbally and non-verbally, and ask clarifying questions to confirm what you have heard.

The second skill is known as empathic listening, which is a form of active listening where you seek to read between the lines and understand the other person's emotional experience. This requires you to temporarily put your thoughts and emotions aside, let go of the need to be right, and immerse yourself in the other person's reality.

Both of these listening skills are useful when communicating with your partner. The skill that you will likely use more frequently is active listening. However, when engaging in tough conversations or resolving conflict, empathic listening can make your partner feel heard and valued.

Here are a few listening exercises that you can practice to develop these two skills:

- **Mentally prepare yourself to listen:** Take a few minutes to quiet your mind, take a few deep breaths, and recenter yourself before you sit down for a conversation. If there is a lot on your mind, or you are emotionally unavailable to listen, ask to speak about light topics that don't require your full attention or postpone the conversation to a later date.

- **Process the words that are being spoken:** Show appreciation for your partner's message by processing each word or sentence they are communicating. Identify strong words that might allude to hidden emotions or assumptions being made. Understand the impact and weight of what they are saying and why they have chosen to use specific language.

- **Get comfortable with pauses:** Don't be quick to respond after your partner has shared their message. Take a few seconds to allow their message to sink deep into your mind, and then proceed by formulating your opinions. Pausing shows your partner that you are paying attention and take their message seriously.

- **Mirror the message you heard:** Constructive conversations are never about showing superiority or proving why your thoughts are more logical than your partner's. Instead, they are about seeking clarity and making sure both individuals walk away feeling heard. You can do this by paraphrasing the message you heard and mirroring it back to your partner to confirm whether you have understood it correctly.

When listening to your partner, consider the fact that behind their message is an idea, belief, or emotion they wish to express to you. Creating a safe space for them to share this idea, belief, or emotion can build trust and a stronger emotional connection. What they need from you isn't always validation, but the willingness to create an environment where they can share pleasant and unpleasant thoughts and emotions without reservation.

Navigating Differences

There is a prevailing myth in society that couples who don't argue have the strongest relationships. The presence of tension or disagreements in relationships is seen as red flags or signs of incompatibility. The truth is that the absence of arguments is not a good thing. It signals a lack of trust, safety, and vulnerability, which makes one or both partners feel afraid or reluctant to speak their minds, share opinions, and express needs and concerns.

Conflict in relationships is normal due to the merging of two separate identities and the different mindsets, histories, and expectations that individuals might bring. You are not expected to agree with every suggestion your partner makes or adopt the same beliefs as them. Thinking and feeling the same as your partner does not strengthen your emotional connection. On the contrary, too much "sameness" can lead to enmeshment and codependency, where both of you lose touch with your needs as individuals.

My clients laugh when I encourage them to fight with their partners. The type of fighting I'm referring to is constructive conflicts that allow for a deeper understanding of your partner's needs. I do not condone destructive conflicts that promote aggressive and manipulative behaviors. These fights don't add any value to your relationship.

Nobody is born knowing how to fight fair and resolve conflict amicably. These conflict resolution skills are often taught by conscious parents, sports coaches, lecturers at the tertiary school level, or leadership training in the workplace. Effective conflict resolution is about acknowledging and defining the problem, looking for common ground, and finding solutions that can work for both parties.

If you are having destructive conflicts with your partner, you are likely to get stuck at one of the three conflict resolution stages. For example, your fights might revolve around the first stage, where you acknowledge and define the problem. You might go back and forth with each other, shifting the blame and targeting each other's characters rather than identifying the troublesome pattern of behavior. Defensive communication and a lack of accountability can make it difficult to move past the problem and proceed to the second stage of looking for common ground.

Getting stuck on the second stage means that neither of you are willing to negotiate. Perhaps you both feel a strong need to be right and have control of the argument. The refusal to negotiate can also be a power play that is used to communicate unmet emotional needs, such as the need for security or autonomy. In other words, both of you may need to assess whether your reluctance to compromise is based on stubbornness or deeper unmet needs. If it is the latter, pause the conflict resolution and prioritize talking about and responding to the unmet needs.

Some couples successfully get through the first and second stages of conflict resolution but get stuck on the final stage where solutions are needed. When this happens, there are usually commitment issues at play.

For example, due to the breakdown of trust, one person may not feel motivated to propose or implement solutions. Alternatively, one person may not bring solutions to the table because they don't see themselves as being responsible for the conflict. This behavior shows that they are operating from an "I" and "me" mentality instead of an "us" and "we" mentality.

There are three strategies that you can practice to ensure positive and constructive conflict resolution:

Focus on the Issue at Hand

It is easy to get distracted by other secondary issues when discussing a particular problem. However, moving from one issue to another can be emotionally draining and makes both of you less motivated to apply your minds to finding a solution for the current issue at hand. Set a rule in your relationship that one issue is raised and resolved during one conversation. If other issues emerge, schedule a time to discuss them in future conversations.

Another tip is to focus on the specific situation that is brought into question instead of analyzing each other's characters. Unless the root issue is your partner's attitude or conduct, you should not be psycho-analyzing them. Both of you should be working together to root out the recurring problem or disagreement that takes place in your relationship.

Avoid Shifting Blame

Sometimes, confronting the issue involves admitting when you were wrong. Owning your part in the situation is not a sign of guilt or weakness. It shows your willingness to de-escalate the conflict, take responsibility for your actions, and be open to learning from your mistakes.

Take a moment to listen to your partner's experience and how they may have been impacted by your actions (or lack of action). Put yourself in their shoes and imagine how they may have processed your behaviors. Acknowledge your oversights by offering an apology and expressing regret for how your behaviors may have contributed to the root issue.

Create an Emotionally Safe Space

It is important for your partner to genuinely feel like you want to listen and understand where they are coming from. For them to feel this way, they must feel validated in your presence. Validating your partner involves being open to what they have to say and allowing them to speak without showing disapproval or defensiveness.

Practice reserving your judgment until you have allowed your partner to share their thoughts and emotions. However, even then, take a minute or so to reflect on what they have shared with you and seek clarity before expressing your thoughts and emotions. Creating an emotionally safe space is not about being a "yes" man or woman who agrees with everything your partner says. It is simply about creating enough space for both of you to speak your minds without anyone feeling afraid.

Silent Conversations

Part of learning your partner's love language involves exploring the nuances of non-verbal communication. It is about discovering the different messages they convey through physical touch, facial expressions, or gestures.

Your partner may not be outspoken or comfortable expressing their thoughts and feelings using words, all the time. However, this doesn't mean they are not committed to keeping the lines of communication open. They may have unspoken cues that reveal what they are thinking or feeling. On the contrary, you may be the introverted partner who prefers speaking through silent conversations. When your partner listens and responds to your non-verbal cues, you can feel seen and validated.

There are four different ways couples can have silent conversations:

Physical Touch

Physical touch is a primary love language for many people in relationships. It is characterized by loving forms of touch like kissing, hand-holding, and cuddling that communicate affection and closeness. For example, stroking your partner's back can be a way to show support without saying the words, "I am here for you." The lack of avoidance of physical touch can communicate opposite feelings of mistrust, insecurity, and feeling disconnected.

Gestures and Posture

Body gestures and posture can be used to validate or invalidate someone. For example, sitting with your arms crossed while listening to your partner shows defensiveness, whereas nodding or slightly tilting your head conveys empathy and compassion. How you position your body (i.e. leaning in while listening or mirroring their actions) can show that you are interested and receptive to what they have to say. Closed gestures and positioning your body away from your partner can be received as rejection or disinterest.

Facial Expressions

Some people express themselves using a variety of positive and negative facial expressions. For example, they frown or tighten their lip when angry, or raise their eyebrows when showing interest or communicating happiness. For shy people, a loving gaze can be a way to communicate affection or sexual desire. On the other hand, a passive-aggressive communicator might give a cold or detached stare when communicating a boundary or showing disapproval. The more emotionally attuned you are to your partner, the easier it will be for you to read the emotions on their face.

Personal Space and Proximity

When couples invite each other into their personal spaces (in the physical and emotional sense) they are communicating the desire to connect and build intimacy. However, there are usually boundaries related to personal space that must be respected for both parties to feel safe in each other's presence. It is important to have discussions around consent and preferences to ensure that both of you feel safe and comfortable having each other within proximity.

If you are a neurodivergent person who finds it difficult to read your partner's non-verbal cues, use the following questions as a guide to understand what they might be thinking or feeling:

- Is your partner making eye contact? Is the eye contact soft and natural, or intense?

- Is your partner showing emotion on their face or giving a blank look? Do they seem emotionally available or distracted?

- Listening to your partner's tone of voice, do they seem calm or irritable? Is their tone respectful or judgmental?

- Is your partner's body stiff or relaxed? Are they facing your direction or looking away?

- Does your partner make physical contact with you? Do they respond positively or negatively to your touch? Do you feel comfortable when touched by your partner?

- How do you feel in your partner's presence? Do they make it easy for you to express yourself? Do you feel wanted in your partner's personal space?

If you are still struggling to pick up on your partner's non-verbal cues, consider the role that technology plays in your communication. How much of your conversations are based on text messages or phone calls rather than face-to-face interactions? Even though technology has become an indispensable part of our lives, it can create barriers to intimacy in romantic relationships. To prevent it from getting in the way of your communication, consider setting a technology curfew if you are living with your partner or planning technology-free dates.

Chapter 7:

My M.E.S.S

You can't always control what goes on outside. But you can always control what goes on inside. —Wayne Dyer

The Role of Self-Esteem

In the previous chapter, we defined and discussed the importance of open communication in healthy romantic relationships. Open communication encourages you to share your thoughts and emotions in a manner that is acceptable and respectful of your partner, and vice versa. As mentioned, it isn't about what you say, but how you deliver the message that matters most.

While open communication can help you address needs and concerns related to your mental, emotional, sexual, and spiritual well-being, it cannot change the way you feel about yourself. For example, if many of the arguments you have with your partner are based on internal insecurities and trust issues, improving your communication won't erase these issues. You need another strategy to target and address them, like building positive self-esteem.

Self-esteem is defined as the perceptions you have about yourself. When these perceptions are balanced (i.e., being able to see both good and bad traits), we say that you have healthy self-esteem, and when they are distorted (i.e. only seeing good or bad traits) we say you have unhealthy self-esteem.

Even though it is normal at times to sink into a pool of self-pity and think poorly about yourself, especially after a sudden loss, failure, or disappointment, entertaining thoughts that constantly pull you down should not become your default. Generally speaking, healthy self-esteem is achieved when you have a fair and balanced view of who you are, considering both failures and accomplishments, strengths and weaknesses.

How Self-Esteem Affects Relationships

For a relationship to work, it must be built and nurtured by two individuals. The responsibilities of fulfilling needs, listening, empathizing, and compromising are shared between a couple. This creates a healthy give-and-take dynamic where both individuals feel satisfied and appreciated by their significant other.

A partner with unhealthy self-esteem is constantly fighting internal battles with themselves and therefore doesn't have much time or motivation to focus on their partner. They may be carrying trauma and emotional baggage from past relationships, which has distorted how they view themselves. These internal battles can feel more real than reality itself, and consume a lot of their mental and emotional energy.

For example, a lady with body issues might avoid being naked in front of her partner because she feels judged or embarrassed. This insecurity prevents her from listening and responding to her partner's need for intimacy, thereby failing to "give" into the relationship. It doesn't matter how much reassurance her partner may offer to challenge these body issues. What she is convinced to be true carries more weight than reality.

Partners with self-esteem issues can come across as selfish because they put their fears and phobias before their significant other's needs. Subsequently, they enter relationships with their guard up and expect to receive affection and everything that comes with a loving union, without making a mental, emotional, sexual, and spiritual investment. Over time, the lack of giving can build resentment and become emotionally draining for the partner who is investing without getting anything in return.

The selfish behavior is only the symptom of a much bigger psychological issue. Partners with unhealthy self-esteem typically have experienced severe pain in the past that has led to a collapse of their identity. Due to past trauma or loss, they have questions about who they are, what they believe to be true, and whether or not they are worthy of giving and receiving affection.

All of these questions create internal conflict and confusion, which is expressed outwardly as coldness, moodiness, perfectionism, commitment issues, self-doubt, pessimistic thinking, or superficial behaviors. In some cases, it can also lead to mental health problems like anxiety, bipolar disorder, and depression, or personality disorders like narcissistic or borderline personality disorder.

To summarize a partner with unhealthy self-esteem, we can say that they have an unstable sense of who they are that causes them to spend more time wrestling with thoughts in their head than being present in the moment. As a result, being in a relationship with them can feel lonely and frustrating because of the lack of give-and-take that is necessary for both people to feel valued.

Self-Esteem-Building Activities

The good news is that self-esteem issues can be addressed through soul-searching activities that inspire greater self-awareness. When you take the time to discover and appreciate who you are, you can start to see your life as being made up of both pleasant and unpleasant experiences. These experiences shape your beliefs and outlooks, but they do not singularly define who you are.

Self-esteem-building activities like the ones listed below help you move away from defining yourself by single events or experiences (i.e. a painful childhood) or viewing yourself in black-or-white terms (i.e. being good or bad, ugly or beautiful, etc.). They encourage you to broaden your self-perception so that you can explore different ideas about who you are, rather than being fixed on a single idea.

Positive Affirmations

Positive affirmations are positive statements recited repeatedly to correct negative thinking and develop a fair and balanced view of yourself. What makes them effective is that they combat negative patterns of thinking by planting positive suggestions in the mind. The more targeted and relevant your affirmations are, the more likely your brain will believe them to be true. For example, telling yourself "I am a millionaire" when you don't have more than $100 in your bank account is not enough to convince your brain that you have the potential to be wealthy. A better affirmation would be, "I am successful at everything I do."

A few things are important to note when creating affirmations from scratch. The first is to write your statements in the present tense, using positive language. The second is to make the statement believable so that your mind doesn't resist the idea. Lastly, your affirmations should be written with your ideal self in mind. Visualize the kind of individual or romantic partner you want to become, and speak as though you are already that person.

Here is a list of positive affirmations to recite daily:

- I deserve to be loved.

- I am capable of expressing love.
- I accept who I am.
- I am beautiful.
- I am comfortable in my own skin.
- I am a pleasure to be around.
- I make myself happy.
- I am a blessing.
- I believe in true love.
- Peace flows through me.
- I am a magnet for healthy relationships.

Learning From Past Experiences

Another great way to improve self-esteem is to learn from past mistakes. Many self-esteem issues are caused by negative thinking or negative self-talk. When you are confronted with a challenge that makes you feel vulnerable, your default is to think poorly about yourself. To correct this, you can reflect on past situations where you thought negatively about yourself and think of better ways to approach similar situations in the future.

The following journaling exercise will help you introspect and confront your patterns of thinking:

1. Describe a recent situation in your relationship where you felt vulnerable.

2. What did you say to yourself about the situation?

3. What negative self-beliefs were triggered?

4. What actions did you immediately take, or feel like taking?

5. What healthy coping behaviors could have changed the outcome of the situation?

6. What encouraging words or affirmations could you have repeated to yourself to prevent negative spiraling thoughts?

7. What unmet emotional need did the situation reveal?

8. What empowering actions can you take next time to respond to your unmet emotional need?

Self-Appreciation

Practicing self-acceptance can help you build healthy self-esteem. Self-acceptance refers to embracing both pleasant and unpleasant aspects of who you are. Instead of highlighting personal attributes that you believe are "normal" and rejecting those that you believe aren't, you are challenged to look at yourself as a unique human being who cannot be benchmarked or compared to a social standard. You simply are who you are, and that is what makes you interesting!

The following journal prompts promote self-discovery and self-appreciation. They encourage you to consider both strengths and weaknesses, fears and desires. As you complete them, adopt a non-judgmental perspective that allows you to think outside the box.

1. What makes me smile is...

____

____

____

2. I have always wanted to...

3. My favorite childhood memory is...

4. My worst childhood memory is...

5. I feel strong when...

6. I am secretly afraid of...

7. My dream is to one day...

8. I find it difficult to admit...

9. One thing people don't know about me is...

10. I feel loved when...

Balancing Togetherness and Independence

Remember that unhealthy self-esteem is caused by an unstable sense of who you are. If you are not feeling stable and confident in yourself, spending a lot of time with your partner can lead to codependency, where you rely on them to make you feel whole. To rebuild self-esteem, you owe it to yourself to balance togetherness with independence in your relationship, so you can cultivate a separate identity from your partner.

Couples naturally desire to spend time together. This is a healthy sign of deepening an emotional connection.

Nevertheless, time together should not come at the cost of individual needs and well-being. In other words, spending time with your partner should not cause you to neglect your own life.

Losing yourself in a relationship is a real issue that couples face. Even though it sounds romantic to merge identities with your partner, a toxic dynamic is created where neither of you can function at your full potential when you are apart. Furthermore, the dynamic causes you to abandon your needs, hide your true emotions, forget about your boundaries, and feel incapable of making decisions about your life.

A certain amount of independence is needed in healthy relationships to reduce pressure and expectations from your partner and maintain a strong sense of self. To function as a whole and stable person, you need some level of autonomy and the ability to express your individuality. Of course, this doesn't mean that you live two lives: one as a single person and another as someone in a partnership. Your loyalty is still with your partner; however, you ensure that you don't lose sight of who you are.

Striking a good balance between time spent together and apart will improve the quality of your relationship. Instead of depending on each other for emotional stability, you both take responsibility for practicing self-care and responding to personal needs. Plus, exploring interests outside your relationship can give you so many things to talk about and bond over when you reunite.

Here are some practices you can work on as a couple to help each other balance togetherness and independence:

- **Communicate your personal needs:** Have open discussions with your partner about personal needs that you would like to focus on. For example, you may be suffering from burnout and need time off work or feel a lack of social connection and need time with your friends.

- **Set healthy boundaries:** Set personal limits regarding your physical space, time investment, mental and emotional health, and so on. Realize that it is okay to not be as open, generous, or social as your partner. For example, it is okay to refuse an invitation and stay home when your partner goes out to socialize.

- **Be intentional about spending quality time:** To make your partner less anxious about being away from you, make sure that you dedicate time to spend together. Ideally, you should be spending more time together than apart; however, if this isn't possible, schedule quality time in advance and ensure you are both comfortable with the arrangements.

- **Find hobbies and personal interests:** Outside of work, find recreational hobbies and interests to stimulate your mind, network with other people, and adopt healthy habits. These hobbies can also help you destress and release tension so that you don't dump emotions on your partner.

- **Set personal goals and aspirations:** Apart from your couple goals, have a few personal goals that you work toward in your free time. These should be goals that can enhance your well-being and positively benefit your relationship. Share these goals with your partner and allow them to be your accountability coach along the way.

Self-Care as Relationship Care

Your romantic relationship is only as healthy as you are as an individual. When one or both of you are physically, mentally, or emotionally unwell, there are areas of your relationship that suffer. Self-care is the practice of being responsive to your physical mental, emotional, and spiritual needs so that you can improve personal well-being. When you are healthy and your cup is full, you have a lot more energy to invest in your relationship.

How many times have you had arguments with your partner that turned out to be issues related to self-care? A few years ago, I had a man come to see me about relationship problems he was having with his girlfriend. When we delved deeper into the problems, we found that they were due to his inability to say no when he felt overwhelmed.

Another couple came to see me months later about a recurring conflict they were having. The woman, who was a stay-at-home mom, felt neglected by her husband. Upon further investigation, we discovered that the woman didn't have personal hobbies outside of caring for her family. She had invested all of her time and energy into her roles as wife and mother, at the expense of her personal growth.

Prioritizing your well-being can be a form of relationship care. When you feel healthy and balanced, fulfilling your relationship duties won't be seen as something stressful. However, when you put yourself last and fail to respond to your needs, your relationship starts to feel like another burden that you are responsible for.

Making time for yourself shouldn't be done when you are moments away from reaching a state of burnout. Ideally, self-care should be an everyday practice that you incorporate into your routine. Moreover, how you choose to practice self-care doesn't need to be expensive, require you to leave the house, or take up too much of your time. You simply need to find the simplest task to respond to a basic need.

Consider the following self-care suggestions to respond to your physical, mental, emotional, social, and spiritual needs:

Physical Self-Care

Do you get enough physical activity each day? Are you taking good care of your body? To improve your physical health, prevent chronic diseases, and wake up feeling recharged every morning, practice the following self-care activities:

- Get eight hours of uninterrupted sleep.
- Consume a healthy and balanced diet.
- Drink water throughout the day to stay hydrated.
- Stretch your body in the mornings and evenings.
- Take a salt bath to relieve muscle tension.

Mental Self-Care

The state of your mental health determines the quality of your thoughts and feelings. By improving your mental health, you can increase levels of concentration, stabilize your moods, and reduce the risk of developing or worsening mental health conditions. Here are some self-care activities to try:

- Start a journaling practice.

- Listen to a motivational podcast.
- Start a meditation practice.
- Start your mornings with a prayer.
- Enroll in a short online course.

Emotional Self-Care

The task of managing and processing your emotions is your responsibility. Having more control over your emotions can reduce outbursts, triggers, projections, and conflicts in your relationship. To improve your emotional regulation skills, incorporate these self-care activities into your daily routine:

- Talk to a therapist or coach.
- Take prescription medication.
- Practice gratitude.
- Surround yourself with positive people.
- Limit social media consumption.

Social Self-Care

Connecting with other people can be a positive way to manage stress, seek support, and feel a sense of belonging. While your partner means the world to you, they cannot satisfy every need you may have. Some needs are best fulfilled by friends and family. To improve your social connections, practice these self-care activities:

- Go on a coffee date with a friend.
- Join a relevant support group.
- Check on your close family members once a week.
- Schedule a video call with a loved one overseas.
- Attend self-improvement workshops and webinars.

Spiritual Self-Care

Grounding activities that promote moments of reflection and solitude are necessary to stay rooted in the essence of who you are. In this fast-paced world, you need to schedule time to check in with yourself, take deep breaths, and reassess your life. The following self-care activities can help you respond to spiritual needs:

- Spend time in nature.
- Go on a spiritual retreat.
- Review your goals.

- Meditate or attend a church service.
- Volunteer for a worthy cause.

Chapter 8:

Through the M.E.S.S

To be fully seen by somebody, then, and be loved anyhow—this is a human offering that can border on miraculous. —Elizabeth Gilbert

Growth Within a Partnership

In the previous chapter, we discussed the role of healthy self-esteem in building strong romantic relationships. We found that couples who feel satisfied in their unions tend to strike a balance between giving and receiving and being together versus being apart. This doesn't mean that people dealing with trauma and emotional issues can't make good partners. It simply means that their priority should be taking care of their mental and emotional well-being so they have more to give to their significant others.

The final chapter is a continuation of the discussion about self-care; however, this time, we are looking into the future and assessing the impact of personal well-being on the relationship's longevity.

Couples who have been together for more than three years will tell you that the electric chemistry that is felt during the initial stages of a relationship fluctuates as life happens. Being in each other's presence, day in and day out, leads to familiarity and complacency. All the wonderful ideas to connect that were helpful while getting to know them, become boring and mechanical after several repetitions.

When the excitement fades and the relationship reaches a plateau, it is common for couples to point fingers at each other, blaming their counterpart for not putting enough effort into keeping the relationship alive. In reality, nobody is at fault. The staleness and dullness of the relationship is a sign that the couple has completed a season of their relationship and a new version of them is required to enter the next season. Being in a flat relationship is an opportunity to level up and evolve into a better version of yourself. The chemistry between you may be gone, but the love can be revived by focusing on personal growth.

Due to experiencing various life transitions like becoming parents, relocating, working longer hours, or facing trauma and loss, neither you nor your partner can return to who you were when you first met. The experiences that you have overcome have altered your mindset, created new fears and desires, and challenged what you previously accepted as "normal" in a relationship. This means that to maintain your relationship, a journey of self-discovery is necessary so you can reintroduce yourself to your partner and teach them everything you have learned about yourself.

Many couples break up or separate when they enter new seasons of their relationships. The phrase that I frequently hear in my counseling room is, "You are not the same person that you used to be." The expectation for our loved ones to remain the same people we fell in love with is both unfair and unrealistic. As human beings who are naturally evolving, they are going to change. However, this change doesn't have to be seen as something negative.

Tips for Growing Together

Harmonious relationships involve two people growing together. They may not be growing in parallel, but they are going in the same direction. Being open and accepting of your partner's growth, and vice versa, can ensure that you navigate through these difficult periods of your relationship as a team, embracing and celebrating the new version of your partner.

With that said, your personal growth should not be to the detriment of your relationship. Even as you focus on self-discovery, it is important to stay attuned to your partner's needs and show commitment to your relationship through:

- **Emotional presence:** Remain open and responsive to your partner's needs. Show them that you are still emotionally available for them by listening, validating their feelings, and being flexible.

- **Transparent communication:** Be honest about the changes you are going through. Avoid shutting your partner out or being defensive when sharing your thoughts and emotions. Remember, how you deliver a message is more important than the content of the message.

- **Mutual respect:** Accept that your partner may not share the same beliefs and values as you. Respect the differences between you and connect over similarities. If your partner is not pursuing personal growth, respect their journey and continue supporting them regardless.

The speed and approach to personal growth may be different for you and your partner. To avoid disappointment and unnecessary conflicts, learn to manage your expectations about what growth should look like. Focus on your transformation and becoming a better partner for your significant other.

Building a Legacy of Love

An encouraging mindset to explore when nurturing a long-term relationship is building a legacy of love. From this view, the purpose of your relationship is not merely to grow old together but to become a model to your friends, family, or children about what enduring and healthy romantic love looks like.

You may not have come from a household where you saw healthy love. You may have been raised by traumatized or mentally ill parents who were unable to display healthy and consistent expressions of love to you. Or perhaps due to their emotional baggage, your parents chose abusive or unsupportive partners and formed a toxic romantic relationship.

Alternatively, you may have been raised in a healthy and loving home but found yourself in a relationship with someone who came from a dysfunctional family. The impact of their personal history and unresolved emotional issues may have created unique challenges in your romantic relationship.

The opportunity presented to you both is to redefine what love means to you and how men and women should relate to and take care of each other in loving relationships. The fact that you didn't grow up with a healthy model of what love is should motivate you to develop a new mindset and set of habits, which you can pass down to your children or positively influence friends and family within your community.

Building a legacy of love is about making a positive impact in the world by correcting unhealthy patterns of behavior within your relationship. As a couple, you can play your role in changing the narrative about modern dating by modeling the M.E.S.S pillars within your relationship. You have the power to make singles, young people, or those in unhappy relationships believe in true love by showing them that it does exist and can be developed through intentional practices.

Conclusion

When we love, we always strive to become better than we are. When we strive to become better than we are, everything around us becomes better too. —Paulo Coelho

Sowing Seeds of Change

When I initially introduced my clients to the M.E.S.S pillars, many were apprehensive about whether they would work or not. They had been in unhealthy relationships for a long time and had not experienced any kind of lasting transformation. Instead of giving a sales pitch and telling them that the pillars would work within x amount of time, I decided to be frank and let them know that the pillars would only work if the seeds of change were planted.

When you plant a seed in the ground, it doesn't evolve into a tree overnight. You must devote yourself to watering the ground and nurturing the soil for months before any signs of life can show. The lack of fruit doesn't mean that there isn't any progress happening below the surface. Following the M.E.S.S pillars is like planting seeds of a healthy and fulfilling relationship in the ground. The results may not be immediate, but that doesn't mean that change isn't happening.

It takes time, practice, and patience to undo harmful relationship habits and build a strong emotional and spiritual connection with your partner. The process is even longer when one or both of you have unresolved trauma and emotional issues to address. Nevertheless, you should not judge your progress by how much time and effort you are investing. Instead, judge your progress by the small changes you notice in your partner's behaviors and the overall satisfaction you feel about your relationship.

The purpose of the four pillars is to bring to your attention the importance of mental, emotional, sexual, and spiritual well-being to build healthy relationships. Nowadays, these fundamental aspects of a relationship are lost in translation due to the prevalence of online dating, casual sex, the culture of perfectionism and comparisons, and manipulative tendencies in relationships. By unlearning what you know about dating and marriage and rebuilding the foundation of your relationship on these four pillars, you can cultivate true love and design the relationship of your dreams.

The best time to get started cleaning up your M.E.S.S is right now. Apply the strategies and knowledge you have learned in this book to deepen the connection with your partner. Start having insightful conversations, validating each other's needs, and redefining what intimacy means and looks like for you. Don't be afraid to disagree with each other; you are not expected to think or feel the same way. What's important is showing empathy, practicing open communication, finding common ground, and pursuing continual growth.

It is also worth emphasizing that this journey is about you just as much as it is about improving your romantic relationship. By seeking to become a better partner, you are encouraged to confront your habits and beliefs, develop emotional intelligence, and practice self-love. Accepting yourself leads to greater acceptance of your relationship and being open to giving and receiving love.

Do you have the courage to confront and realign the M.E.S.S in your relationship? This transformative experience is available to you, right now!

References

A guide to productively communicating your feelings. (2019, February 13). Psych Company. https://www.psychcompany.com/productively-communicating-your-feelings/

AAMFT. (2015). *About marriage and family therapists.* AAMFT. https://www.aamft.org/About_AAMFT/About_Marriage_and_Family_Therapists.aspx

Ackerman, C. E. (2017, May 23). *18 best self-esteem worksheets and activities (incl. PDF).* Positive Psychology. https://positivepsychology.com/self-esteem-worksheets/#adults-self-esteem

And benching: The unsettling trends of modern dating. (2023, October 17). Faster Capital. https://fastercapital.com/content/And-Benching--The-Unsettling-Trends-of-Modern-Dating.html

Angelou, M. (2023, June 15). *123 funny & cute relationship quotes that every couple can relate to.* Hitched. https://www.hitched.co.uk/wedding-planning/organising-and-planning/relationship-quotes/

Brandt, A. (2018, April 2). *9 steps to healing childhood trauma as an adult.* Psychology Today. https://www.psychologytoday.com/za/blog/mindful-anger/201804/9-steps-healing-childhood-trauma-adult

Brickel, R. E. (2016, April 28). *Loving a trauma survivor: Understanding childhood trauma's impact on relationships.* PsychAlive. https://www.psychalive.org/loving-trauma-survivor-understanding-childhood-traumas-impact-relationships/#:~:text=Seeing%20Trauma

Bronson, M. (2019, November 2). *Characteristics of a healing relationship.* Phoenix Society. https://www.phoenix-society.org/resources/characteristics-of-a-healing-relationship

Bueti, G. (2022, September 22). Love bombing can feel A lot like romance — here's how to tell them apart. *Refinery29.* https://www.refinery29.com/en-gb/what-is-love-bombing

C. JoyBell C. (2023, June 15). *123 funny & cute relationship quotes that every couple can relate to.* Hitched. https://www.hitched.co.uk/wedding-planning/organising-and-planning/relationship-quotes/

Cherry, K. (2022, September 20). *Why cultivating a growth mindset can boost your success.* Verywell Mind.

https://www.verywellmind.com/what-is-a-mindset-2795025

Chiy, A. (2023, August 15). *"Partnership dynamics: Navigating relationship responsibilities with a growth mindset."* LinkedIn. https://www.linkedin.com/pulse/partnership-dynamics-navigating-relationship-growth-mindset-chiy/?trk=public_post

Coehlo, P. (2022, July 11). *150 cute relationship quotes that'll get you in your feelings.* Woman's Day. https://www.womansday.com/relationships/g20888175/relationship-quotes/

de Saint-Exupery, A. (2023, June 15). *123 Funny and cute relationship quotes that every couple can relate to.* Hitched. https://www.hitched.co.uk/wedding-planning/organising-and-planning/relationship-quotes/

Dyer, W. (n.d.). *51 self care quotes and tiny reminders to love yourself.* Fortune and Frame. https://fortuneandframe.com/blogs/news/self-care-quotes

Easterly, E. (2022, April 25). *Forgiveness as a spiritual practice.* Chopra. https://chopra.com/articles/forgiveness-as-a-spiritual-practice

Edwards, S. (2015). *Love and the brain.* Harvard Medical School. https://hms.harvard.edu/news-events/publications-archive/brain/love-brain

Eldemire, A. (2019, September 24). *How mental illness affects romantic relationships.* Psychology Today South Africa. https://www.psychologytoday.com/za/blog/couples-thrive/201909/how-mental-illness-affects-romantic-relationships

Epicurus. (2023, June 15). *123 funny & cute relationship quotes that every couple can relate to.* Hitched. https://www.hitched.co.uk/wedding-planning/organising-and-planning/relationship-quotes/

Epp Buckingham, J. (2012). *The relationship between religions and a secular society.* Ontario Human Rights Commission. https://www.ohrc.on.ca/en/creed-freedom-religion-and-human-rights-special-issue-diversity-magazine-volume-93-summer-2012/relationship-between-religions-and-secular-society

Examples of cognitive restructuring. (n.d.). Concordia University. https://www.concordia.ca/cunews/offices/provost/health/topics/stress-management/cognitive-restructuring-examples.html

Field, B. (2023, February 21). *What is sexual chemistry?* Verywell Mind. https://www.verywellmind.com/what-is-sexual-chemistry-all-about-5210910#toc-how-sexual-chemistry-develops

Gheorgheza, C. (2023, November 7). *Understanding love languages through body language.* LinkedIn. https://www.linkedin.com/pulse/understanding-love-languages-through-body-language-corina-gheorgheza-r5mme/

Gilbert, E. (2022, July 11). *150 cute relationship quotes that'll get you in your feelings.* Woman's Day. https://www.womansday.com/relationships/g20888175/relationship-quotes/

Gillis, K. (2022, February 19). *10 ways childhood trauma can manifest in adult relationships.* Psychology Today South Africa. https://www.psychologytoday.com/za/blog/invisible-bruises/202202/10-ways-childhood-trauma-can-manifest-in-adult-relationships

Gillis, K. (2023, August 15). *Spiritual intimacy: What it is and how to build it in relationships.* Choosing Therapy. https://www.choosingtherapy.com/spiritual-intimacy/

Graham, J. (2013, August 6). *down with (patriarchal) love.* Young Mormon Feminists. https://youngmormonfeminists.org/2013/08/06/down-with-patriarchal-love/

Greatness Authors. (2023, August 8). *Get in sync with your partner.* Greatness. https://greatness.com/get-in-sync-with-your-partner/

Gupta, S. (2023, June 20). *What does the term "emotional baggage" mean?* Verywell Mind.

https://www.verywellmind.com/emotional-baggage-symptoms-causes-and-coping-strategies-6742778

Harris, V. W. (2018, March 9). *10 rules for constructive conflict.* University of Florida. https://edis.ifas.ufl.edu/publication/FY1276

Herrity, J. (2023, July 31). *5 effective conflict resolution strategies.* Indeed Career Guide. https://www.indeed.com/career-advice/career-development/conflict-resolution-strategies

Hickman, R. (2020, February 12). *The importance of silence in relationships.* Pathways Professional. https://www.pathwaysprofessional.org/blog/2020/2/12/the-importance-of-silence-in-relationships#:~:text=Healthy%20silence%20can%20show%20a

Jarvis, S. (2018, February 6). *Sexual problems - how to talk to your partner about sex.* Patient. https://patient.info/news-and-features/how-to-talk-to-your-partner-about-a-sexual-problem

Johnson, M. B. (2020, December 9). *400+ deep intimacy quotes for him and her.* MomJunction. https://www.momjunction.com/articles/intimacy-quotes_00685979/

Krauss Whitbourne, S. (2023, April 1). *How important is it to be in sync with a partner?* Psychology Today. https://www.psychologytoday.com/intl/blog/fulfillment-at-any-age/202303/is-it-always-good-to-be-in-sync-with-your-partner

Lancer, D. (2016, February 28). *Self-esteem and relationships: How one affects the other.* Psych Central. https://psychcentral.com/lib/self-esteem-makes-successful-relationships#Communication-Reveals-Self-Esteem

Lancer, D. (2019, June 18). *A relationship as a spiritual path.* Psych Central. https://psychcentral.com/lib/a-relationship-as-a-spiritual-path

Landau, E. (2016, February 8). *Commitment for millennials: Is it okay, cupid?* Scientific American Blog Network. https://blogs.scientificamerican.com/mind-guest-blog/commitment-for-millennials-is-it-okay-cupid/

Le, T. N. (2005). Narcissism and immature love as mediators of vertical individualism and ludic love style. *Journal of Social and Personal Relationships*, *22*(4), 543–560. https://doi.org/10.1177/0265407505054522

Loewen, W. (2017, October 20). *6 steps for constructive conflict resolution.* Achieve Centre. https://achievecentre.com/blog/6-steps-constructive-conflict-resolution/

Magee, D. (2019, November 18). *Understanding the dating scene: Modern vs. traditional approaches.* The Sundial. https://sundial.csun.edu/155577/arts-entertainment/understanding-the-dating-scene-modern-vs-traditional-approaches/

Mangat, S. (2020, August 28). *6 hallmarks of feminist relationships.* Feminism in India. https://feminisminindia.com/2020/08/28/6-hallmarks-of-feminist-relationships/

Manson, M. (2013, April 11). *Sex and our psychological needs.* Mark Manson. https://markmanson.net/sex-and-our-psychological-needs

May, R. (2021, March 24). *75 communication quotes and sayings to strengthen relationships.* Everyday Power. https://everydaypower.com/communication-quotes-and-sayings/

Meji, O. (2018, August 24). *12 signs of spiritual compatibility in relationships.* Embracing Spirituality. https://www.embracingspirituality.com/2018/08/24/12-signs-of-spiritual-compatibility-in-relationships/

Moul, R. (2023, April 3). *Polyamory is on the rise and society should be more accommodating, research argues.* IFLScience. https://www.iflscience.com/polyamory-is-on-the-rise-and-society-should-be-more-accommodating-research-argues-68281

O'Donohue, J. (2019, February 28). *50 spiritual quotes to help you feel divinely connected.* Fortunate Goods. https://fortunategoods.com/blogs/articles/spirituality-quotes

Onele, A. (2021, April 5). *Mental models; shape your future?* LinkedIn. https://www.linkedin.com/pulse/mental-models-shape-austin-onele/?trk=public_profile_article_view

Past sexual trauma affecting your relationships. (2019, January 6). Vantage Point Recovery. https://vantagepointrecovery.com/past-sexual-trauma/#:~:text=Finding%20treatment%20or%20an%20individual

Peterson, R. (2022, September 1). *Creating a legacy of love.* Growing Marriages. https://www.growingmarriages.org/creating-a-legacy-of-love/

Popova, T., & Wiese, H. (2022). The time it takes to truly know someone: Neurophysiological correlates of face and identity learning during the first two years. *Biological Psychology*, *170*, 108312. https://doi.org/10.1016/j.biopsycho.2022.108312

Rampton, M. (2015, October 25). *Four waves of feminism.* Pacific University. https://www.pacificu.edu/magazine/four-waves-feminism#:~:text=The%20wave%20formally%20began%20at

Ramsey. (2022, October 4). *How to grow spiritually with your partner.* Ramsey Solutions. https://www.ramseysolutions.com/personal-growth/how-to-grow-spiritually-with-your-partner

Rice, M. (2021, November 19). *13 types of couples therapy techniques.* Talkspace. https://www.talkspace.com/blog/couples-therapy-techniques/

Rosenblatt, K. (2022, September 29). *How to fix a broken relationship [therapist advice].* Talkspace. https://www.talkspace.com/blog/how-to-fix-a-broken-relationship/

Rothberg, S. (2015). *Stages of forgiveness.* Lifeway. https://www.lifeway.com/en/articles/steps-to-forgiveness

Schuler, C. (2022, June 28). *Eight practices that are revolutionizing my marriage.* Biola University. https://cmr.biola.edu/blog/2022/jun/28/eight-practices-are-revolutionizing-my-marriage/

Segal, J., Smith, M., Robinson, L., & Boose, G. (2023, March 1). *Nonverbal communication and body language.* HelpGuide. https://www.helpguide.org/articles/relationships-communication/nonverbal-communication.htm

Seven types of self-care and why you need them. (2021, September 6). Health Coach Institute. https://www.healthcoachinstitute.com/articles/7-types-of-self-care/

Sexual communication. (n.d.). SHCS. https://shcs.ucdavis.edu/health-topic/sexual-communication

Shatto, R. (2018, October 9). *10 soothing activities that you and your partner can enjoy together in silence.* Elite Daily. https://www.elitedaily.com/p/10-silent-things-to-do-with-your-boyfriend-girlfriend-when-you-need-down-time-12188253

Smith, S. (2022, December 16). *15 common sexual problems in marriage and ways to fix them.* Marriage. https://www.marriage.com/advice/physical-intimacy/how-to-fix-sexual-problems-in-a-marriage/

Smith, S. (2023, March 21). *How to fix a strained relationship.* Marriage. https://www.marriage.com/advice/relationship/strained-relationship/

SoulFacts. (2023, September 23). *Balancing independence and togetherness in relationships.* Medium. https://medium.com/@soul-facts/balancing-independence-and-togetherness-in-relationships-59ce9ff4a714

Spencer, N. (2023, August 9). *The evolution of modern dating: From traditional to digital connections.* Isrg Digi. https://www.isrgrajan.com/digi/the-evolution-of-modern-dating-from-traditional-to-digital-connections.html

Stanborough, R. J. (2023, June 5). *Cognitive restructuring: Techniques and examples.* Healthline.

https://www.healthline.com/health/cognitive-restructuring#gathering-evidence

Szekely, G. (2019, January 6). *Why self-care is so important for longevity and wellness.* The Couples Center. https://www.thecouplescenter.org/why-self-care-is-so-important-for-longevity-and-wellness/

Szekely, G. (2023, July 3). *Healing from sexual trauma in a relationship.* The Couples Center. https://www.thecouplescenter.org/healing-from-sexual-trauma-in-a-relationship/

Tee-Melegrito, R. A. (2023, April 27). *Mismatched sex drives: Relationships and coping.* Medical News Today. https://www.medicalnewstoday.com/articles/mismatched-sex-drives#what-affects-sex-drive

Telloian, C. (2022, September 13). *Intimacy in relationships: Types, roadblocks, and how to build.* Psych Central. https://psychcentral.com/relationships/intimacy-definition-types-tips#recap

Ten cognitive distortions that can ruin relationships. (2016, August 20). Psych Central. https://psychcentral.com/blog/10-cognitive-distortions-that-can-ruin-relationships#1

The 5 communication styles explained (& how to improve yours). (2022, January 27). Project. https://www.project.co/communication-styles/

Vader, K. (2019, August 12). *Emotional intelligence in love and relationships.* HelpGuide. https://www.helpguide.org/articles/mental-health/emotional-intelligence-love-relationships.htm

Waisman, E. (2023, October 5). *Emotional baggage: What are the signs it's holding you back?* Jaunty. https://www.jaunty.org/blog/emotional-baggage

Why developing a spiritual practice is key to living a balanced life. (2019, February 17). A Soulful Rebellion. https://asoulfulrebellion.com/blog/spiritual-practices

Why the link between sex and emotional connection is so important. (n.d.). The Adventure Challenge. https://www.theadventurechallenge.com/blogs/news/sex-and-emotional-connection

Wilson, C. R. (2021, October 29). *How to improve your empathic listening skills: 7 techniques.* Positive Psychology. https://positivepsychology.com/empathic-listening/#empathic-listening

Wooll, M. (2021, August 25). *Finding common ground with anyone.* BetterUp. https://www.betterup.com/blog/finding-common-ground-with-anyone-a-quick-and-easy-guide

Yerkovich, K. (2016, June 17). *How childhood experiences impact love styles.* Focus on the Family.

https://www.focusonthefamily.com/marriage/how-childhood-experiences-impact-marriage-relationships/

Made in the USA
Columbia, SC
13 May 2024

35641373R00114